THE SMALL BUSINESS OWNER'S CYBERSECURITY GUIDE

A COMPREHENSIVE GUIDE TO EASILY PROTECT YOUR
BUSINESS AND CLIENTS ONLINE

TODD MITCHELL

The publication was developed by Todd Mitchell, owner of Cybersecurity4biz, LLC, with input from public and private sector partners, including the National Institute of Standards and Technology (NIST) Cybersecurity Framework (CSF), Health Insurance Portability and Accountability Act (HIPAA), Payment Card Industry Data Security Standard (PCI-DSS) requirements; the NIST Risk Management Framework, Federal Communication Commission, the Department of Homeland Security, the National Cyber Security Alliance, and The US Chamber of Commerce.

Book cover by Todd Mitchell

979-8-9931225-0-2 | Paperback

979-8-9931225-1-9 | Ebook

CONTENTS

PROTECT YOUR BUSINESS WITH A FREE CYBERSECURITY CHECKUP

Take my **Free Cybersecurity Assessment** today and discover how it benefits you:

✅ **See Your Blind Spots** – Quickly find out where hackers could slip in without you realizing it.

✅ **Protect Your Reputation** – Your clients trust you with their information; one breach can break that trust.

✅ **Save Money** – A simple prevention plan now costs pennies compared to the thousands a breach can cost later.

✅ **Stay Compliant** – Learn if your business is meeting requirements like HIPAA, GLBA, PCI-DSS, or CMMC 2.0.

✅ **Peace of Mind** – Know exactly what steps to take so you can stop worrying about "what if" and get back to running your business.

Scan the QR code below or visit:

www.cybersecurity4biz.com/free-assessments

WHY TAKE THIS ASSESSMENT?

- Because the cost of prevention is pennies compared to the cost of a breach.
- **This is 100% free. No strings attached.**
- It's my way of helping solopreneurs, micro businesses, and families stay safe online.

Take the first step now. Protect your business, your customers, and your peace of mind.

Cybersecurity4biz – Because they trust you to protect their information.

DEDICATION

To my loving wife, Tammy, whose strength, sacrifice, and unwavering support made it possible for me to pursue my education and follow this journey. Your encouragement has been the steady foundation that allowed me to keep moving forward.

To my daughter, Amber, and my two grandchildren, who are my pride and joy. You are the reason I strive to grow, improve, and leave behind something meaningful. Your laughter, love, and inspiration remind me daily of why this work matters.

Without each of you, this book would not exist.

INTRODUCTION

WHY CYBERSECURITY MATTERS FOR SOLOPRENEURS AND SMALL BUSINESSES

Imagine walking into your office one morning, coffee in hand, ready to conquer your day. You log in to your business accounts and—nothing. Your data is gone, locked behind a digital ransom note demanding thousands of dollars.

Scary, right?

Unfortunately, this isn't just a nightmare; it's a reality many small businesses face every day. And no, it's not just the big guys being targeted. In fact, **solopreneurs and micro-businesses are often the favorite prey of cybercriminals**, because they tend to have the least protection. It's like leaving your front door wide open with a neon "no alarm system" sign hanging above it.

So why are we on their radar?

Cybercriminals, whether they're bored teenagers, rogue nation-states, or professional crime syndicates, are playing the numbers game. They know that smaller businesses often skip out on cybersecurity basics—either because they don't know where to start or they assume, "Who would want to hack little ol' me?" Well, here's the truth: **you have data, money, and access. That's more than enough motivation**.

Your customer lists, billing systems, tax IDs, login credentials, and even your reputation are digital gold for hackers. Once inside, they can steal, encrypt, delete, or sell your information. And if you serve regulated industries like healthcare or finance? That makes you even more valuable. Attackers know that HIPAA, GLBA, and PCI fines are costly—and you may pay up just to avoid a bigger problem.

But here's the good news: **you don't need a massive IT team or a Silicon Valley budget to fight back**. What you need is a simple, scalable plan, a system to help you stay ahead of the bad guys.

This is where cybersecurity comes in. It's not just about protecting your data; it's about protecting your **reputation**, your **livelihood**, and the **trust your customers place in you**. Cybersecurity is the silent partner in your business success, ensuring you can focus on growth without constantly looking over your digital shoulder.

WHY NIST CSF 2.0 IS YOUR PERFECT FIT

You've probably heard about complex cybersecurity frameworks and wondered if they're just for Fortune 500 companies with entire floors dedicated to IT security. But the National Institute of Standards and Technology's Cybersecurity Framework—aka NIST CSF—is different. It's not a one-size-fits-all straightjacket; it's a **flexible roadmap** that adapts to your business's size, goals, and budget.

The new and improved **NIST CSF 2.0** is built around six simple but powerful functions that anyone can understand—even if your tech skills stop at rebooting your router:

- **Govern** – Establishing rules and accountability for cybersecurity in your business. Who's in charge of what, and what policies do you follow?
- **Identify** – Understanding what you have, what's at risk, and where you're vulnerable. It's like taking inventory of your digital assets and weak spots.
- **Protect** – Putting up the right defenses to keep threats out, like firewalls, encryption, and security training.
- **Detect** – Spotting potential threats before they escalate. Think of this as your digital smoke alarm.
- **Respond** – Knowing what to do when something goes wrong. Because accidents (and hackers) happen.
- **Recover** – Getting back on track quickly and with minimal damage. This is your business continuity and disaster recovery playbook.

In this book, we'll break down each function into clear, actionable steps designed specifically for solopreneurs and small business owners. No tech jargon, no confusing diagrams—just practical advice you can implement right away, even if you think "cybersecurity" sounds like a job for NASA.

HOW THIS BOOK WILL HELP YOU

Cybersecurity doesn't have to be overwhelming. This book is your friendly guide to creating a cyber-safe business—without the stress, panic Googling, or waking up at 3 a.m. wondering if your customer database just got breached.

Here's what we'll cover together:

We'll start with the **Core 4 Principles**—daily cybersecurity habits that are easy to do, easy to remember, and make a huge difference. Think of them as brushing your teeth, but for your business: using strong passwords, enabling multi-factor authentication (MFA), keeping your software updated, and learning how to spot phishing scams.

Then, we'll dig into **how to build a cyber-safe culture**— even if you're a one-person show. It's about turning smart security decisions into second nature, not something you only think about after a breach.

You'll also learn how to **measure your cybersecurity ROI**. Yes, cybersecurity actually protects your bottom line—and we'll show you how to connect the dots between prevention and profit.

Finally, we'll walk through a **step-by-step implementation plan** using the NIST CSF 2.0 framework. You'll go at your own pace, customizing your cyber strategy without getting lost in tech-speak or buried under paperwork.

Whether you're a solopreneur juggling client calls from your kitchen table or managing a lean, scrappy team from a co-working space, this book is your roadmap to digital resilience. By the time you've finished, you'll have the tools, knowledge, and confidence to protect your business from cyber threats—and even use cybersecurity as a competitive advantage.

Because let's face it: trust is everything. And in the digital world, cybersecurity is trust in action.

Before we dive in, I want to offer you something that can help you take immediate action. If you're a solopreneur or small business owner and want to know where your cybersecurity stands today, I invite you to get a **free cybersecurity assessment** on my website.

It's quick, non-techy, and tailored for busy folks like you—no geek-speak, I promise. You'll get personalized insights and recommendations based on your specific risks and industry.

Just head to **https://www.cybersecurity4biz.com/free-assessments** to grab your free assessment.

Let's start protecting what you've worked so hard to build.

UNDERSTANDING NIST CSF 2.0 AND THE CORE 4 PRINCIPLES

WHAT IS CYBERSECURITY AND WHY DO YOU NEED IT?

Cybersecurity is like the digital equivalent of locking your doors at night and installing a security system for your home —except instead of protecting your physical belongings, it safeguards your digital assets. And let's be honest, in today's world, our digital assets are often *more valuable* than the physical ones.

These digital assets include everything from customer contact details and financial records to proprietary business data and sensitive health information. If you collect it, store it, or share it—then it needs to be protected. Period.

A. Contact Information

Think about the names, email addresses, phone numbers, and mailing addresses you collect. This data may seem harmless, but it can be weaponized for phishing scams or identity theft.

Regulations: GDPR, CCPA, and most U.S. state privacy laws require you to protect and be transparent about how you use this information.

B. Personal Identification

Details like Social Security Numbers, birth dates, or driver's licenses are the Holy Grail for identity thieves.

Regulations: GLBA, HIPAA, and various state laws mandate businesses to safeguard this data.

C. Income & Tax Information

Your clients' income, tax filings, and financial records? Hackers love this stuff. It's like giving them the blueprint to someone's financial life.

Regulations: GLBA and the IRS Safeguards Rule ensure tax professionals and financial firms keep this info locked down.

D. Financial Information

Bank accounts, credit cards, access codes—this is the cash register of your business. If someone breaches this, they're not just stealing data—they're stealing dollars.

Regulations: GLBA, PCI-DSS, and FCRA come into play here, ensuring businesses secure financial transactions and data.

E. Credentials & Database Information

Usernames, passwords, and business databases are like the keys to your kingdom. If breached, the attacker has full access to the castle.

Regulations: NIST CSF, HIPAA, and GLBA push businesses to tighten access controls.

F. Intellectual Property & Proprietary Business Data

Trade secrets, product designs, and creative content may not seem juicy to a random hacker, but to your competitor—or a cybercriminal looking to sell them on the dark web—they're pure gold.

Regulations: Protected under laws like the DTSA and EEA, as well as any NDAs you've signed.

G. Medical & Health Information

Patient records and health histories are extremely sensitive. A breach here can have devastating consequences—not just for patients, but for your reputation.

Regulations: HIPAA and HITECH Act enforce strict rules for securing electronic health data.

When this kind of information falls into the wrong hands, the consequences can be devastating. Imagine if your customers' personal data were leaked online. You'd face:

- **Loss of Trust:** Customers may leave, feeling betrayed and unsafe.
- **Financial Penalties:** Regulatory fines for failing to protect sensitive data.
- **Operational Disruption:** Time and money spent recovering from the breach.
- **Legal Fallout:** Potential lawsuits from affected customers or partners.

Think of cybersecurity as the shield that protects not only your business but also the people who trust you with their data. By implementing strong defenses, you're sending a clear message: **"Your information is safe with us."**

THE SIX NIST CSF FUNCTIONS: YOUR CYBERSECURITY BLUEPRINT

Cybersecurity may sound complicated, but it's really about following a simple, structured plan. At the heart of this plan are six essential functions that make up the NIST Cybersecurity Framework:

- **Govern:** This is your playbook. You set the rules, assign responsibilities, and make cybersecurity part of the culture. If cybersecurity were football, this is your team huddle where everyone knows their role.
- **Identify:** You can't protect what you don't know you have. This step is about taking inventory—what data do you collect, where is it stored, and what's at risk?
- **Protect:** Now that you know what you have, it's time to defend it. Strong passwords, MFA, firewalls, and encryption, these are the digital locks and alarms on your business.
- **Detect:** Monitoring unusual behavior is key. If someone's creeping around your digital backyard at 2 a.m., you want to know about it—*before* they break in.
- **Respond:** When something goes wrong (because someday, it will), you need a plan. Quick, smart

action can contain the damage and show your clients you've got things under control.

- **Recover:** Bounce back and learn. This step is about restoring your systems and improving your defenses so you're stronger next time—like patching the roof after a storm, and adding a lightning rod while you're at it.

We'll unpack each of these functions further in the coming chapters, so you'll always know what to do and when.

THE CORE 4 PRINCIPLES FOR EVERYDAY CYBERSECURITY

While the NIST Cybersecurity Framework provides an excellent high-level strategy for managing risk, the Core 4 principles are what you use day in and day out to actually stay safe. These are the personal habits and digital hygiene routines that, when done consistently, form a solid first line of defense against common cyber threats. Think of these as your daily health habits—brushing your teeth, locking your doors, and washing your hands—but for your digital life.

1. Use Multi-Factor Authentication (MFA)

Multi-Factor Authentication, or MFA, adds a critical layer of security to your online accounts. It works by requiring more than one piece of information to verify your identity, typically something you know (like a password) and something you have (like a smartphone or a hardware token). Even if a hacker gets your password, they'll still be blocked unless they also have your second factor.

The reason MFA is so powerful is that it significantly reduces the risk of unauthorized access. Passwords are often compromised through phishing emails, data breaches, or social engineering tactics. But with MFA in place, a stolen password alone isn't enough to access your sensitive information. Think of it like locking your door and also installing a security system. It may take an extra few seconds to log in, but that small inconvenience offers a major security payoff.

To make the most of MFA, enable it on all critical accounts, including email, banking, healthcare portals, and any platform that contains personal or business information. Choose an authenticator app over text message codes when available, as apps are more secure and less vulnerable to SIM-swapping attacks.

2. Create Strong Passwords and Use Unique Accounts

Passwords are often the only thing standing between a hacker and your sensitive information. Unfortunately, many people still use short, simple, and reused passwords that can be easily guessed or cracked. A strong password is long, random, and unique to each account. Instead of using your dog's name or your birthdate, use a passphrase that combines unrelated words, symbols, and numbers—something like "Coffee-Table!Rain47Walk."

Just as important as strong passwords is the habit of using different passwords for different accounts. When you reuse passwords across websites, a breach at one site can lead to a domino effect. Cybercriminals use automated tools to test stolen login credentials across hundreds of sites, a tactic known as credential stuffing. If you reuse passwords, one breach can give them access to everything.

A password manager can help make this easier. It securely stores your login information, generates strong passwords for you, and auto-fills them when needed. This removes the burden of memorization while maintaining a high level of security.

3. Keep Your Software Updated

Software updates aren't just about getting new features or fixing bugs; they often include security patches that protect you from known vulnerabilities. Hackers actively scan the internet for outdated software they can exploit. These vulnerabilities are like open windows into your systems, and an update is essentially slamming that window shut.

Unfortunately, many people delay or ignore update prompts out of convenience or fear of breaking something. But putting off updates is like refusing to patch a leak in your roof because it's not raining yet. The longer you wait, the greater the risk becomes.

To stay ahead of the threats, set your devices to automatically install updates whenever possible. This includes your operating system, web browsers, antivirus programs, and even things like your home Wi-Fi router or smart devices. And don't forget your mobile apps—particularly banking, health, and email apps—which often contain sensitive data. For peace of mind, set aside time once a month to check for manual updates and clean up any unused apps or software.

4. Recognize Social Engineering Attacks

Social engineering is one of the most effective methods hackers use to breach your defenses, and it doesn't require any technical skill. Instead of breaking through your firewalls, they try to trick you into opening the door for them. The most common form of this is phishing, where attackers send emails, texts, or pop-ups that appear legitimate but are designed to steal your information or infect your device.

These messages often create a false sense of urgency—telling you that your account is locked, your payment failed, or there's a security alert that requires immediate action. They rely on fear, curiosity, or confusion to get you to click a link or share personal information without thinking twice. Once you click, the damage may already be done.

The best defense is awareness. Pause and think before clicking on anything that seems out of the ordinary. Look closely at the sender's email address, the language used, and any unusual formatting. If you're ever unsure whether a message is legitimate, go directly to the source; don't use the contact information provided in the message. Instead, log into your account through a trusted browser or call the company using a verified number.

Training yourself to recognize these tricks is essential. You can even keep a collection of fake or suspicious messages as a personal training tool to spot patterns and help educate your team or family members.

BUILDING CYBER-SAFE HABITS

The Core 4 are not difficult, but they do require consistency. By enabling MFA, using strong and unique passwords, keeping your software up to date, and staying alert to social engineering attempts, you're covering the majority of the cybersecurity threats that individuals and small businesses face every day.

These aren't one-time tasks; they're habits. The more you incorporate them into your routine, the less you'll have to worry about someone sneaking into your digital life. In the end, cybersecurity isn't about paranoia; it's about prevention, awareness, and keeping the keys to your kingdom firmly in your hands.

By combining these principles with the NIST CSF framework, you'll have both the big-picture strategy and the daily habits you need to stay secure. Together, they act like a fortress—one where you're not just the owner but the commander, architect, and protector.

BUILDING A CYBER-SAFE BUSINESS CULTURE

WHY CULTURE MATTERS MORE THAN TECHNOLOGY

When it comes to cybersecurity, the tools you use—like firewalls, antivirus software, and encryption—are only part of the story. They provide the armor, but the real strength of your defense lies in behavior. Your daily habits, along with the habits of your team (even if it's just you and a contractor), are what truly make or break your cybersecurity efforts.

Consider this: over eighty percent of data breaches are caused by human error. Cybercriminals know this, and they bank on it. They rely on manipulation—through phishing, social engineering, and other psychological tricks—to bypass even the most secure systems. That's why a strong cybersecurity culture matters. A business with clear habits and ongoing awareness is like a well-fortified castle. One that ignores these practices is more like a house with the front door wide open and a welcome mat that reads, "Take what you want."

CREATING HABITS THAT STICK

Building a cyber-safe culture doesn't mean flipping your business upside down. In fact, it starts with small, consistent actions. Making Multi-Factor Authentication (MFA) mandatory for every account and every login is one of the simplest and most effective first steps. Think of MFA as your digital double-lock system. It's a habit that quickly becomes second nature, and once it's in place, you'll wonder how you ever lived without it.

Another crucial habit is normalizing updates. Software updates often feel like a nuisance, but they're like oil changes for your digital tools. They may not feel urgent at the moment, but neglecting them will cost you down the road—often in ways you can't afford. Encourage yourself and your team to treat updates as routine maintenance, not optional chores.

Finally, cultivate a mindset of skepticism. If something seems off—whether it's an email, a link, or a sudden request—pause before acting. Encourage a culture where questioning is welcomed, and verification is the norm. This doesn't mean living in constant fear; it means training your brain to tap the brakes instead of flooring the gas when something unexpected pops up.

Whether you're a solopreneur or working with a few freelancers, your culture sets the tone. Every person with access to your business systems becomes part of your cybersecurity defense. That means it's critical to share good habits, talk about data handling expectations, and model the behaviors you want others to follow. Lead by example. If you make security a visible priority, those around you are more likely to do the same.

Think of cybersecurity culture like brushing your teeth. One skipped day won't destroy everything, but a habit of neglect over time? That leads to problems you can't ignore. Just like good dental hygiene prevents root canals, daily cyber hygiene prevents costly data disasters.

DEVELOPING POLICIES THAT MAKE SENSE FOR YOUR BUSINESS

While culture sets the tone, policies provide the structure. They're the backbone of a cyber-safe business. Here's the good news: your policies don't have to be long, technical, or filled with legalese. The best ones are simple, clear, and action-able. At a basic level, a good policy answers three questions:hat should I do? How should I do it? And why does it matter?

Take password management, for example. You want a policy that clearly states that all passwords must be strong, with at least 12 characters that include letters, numbers, and symbols. Reusing passwords across accounts should be strictly prohib-ited. Instead, employees and contractors should be instructed to use a password manager to store and generate complex passwords securely. An example of a simple policy might read: "All passwords must be unique and stored in [password manager tool]. Never write passwords on paper or share them via email."

Device security is another must-have area. Your policy should ensure all business devices—laptops, phones, and tablets—are encrypted, password-protected, and set to install software updates automatically. Install endpoint protection tools, such as antivirus software, to add another layer of defense. A sample rule might be: "All business devices must be locked with a secure PIN or password and updated monthly."

And don't forget data handling. Sensitive information, such as customer payment info or medical records, should only be stored in encrypted, secure systems. When data needs to be shared, use secure, encrypted cloud tools—not email. If emailing sensitive data is unavoidable, it must be encrypted and approved beforehand. A policy guideline might say: "Customer data must be shared only via [secure cloud tool]. Emailing sensitive information is not allowed without prior approval."

If you work with freelancers or remote teams, policies become even more important. You must communicate with them clearly and enforce them consistently. Consider creating a one-page cheat sheet that highlights key policies in plain language. Use secure platforms, such as Microsoft Teams or Slack, for collaboration, and make sure contractors sign a confidentiality or cybersecurity agreement before being granted access to your systems.

Keep in mind: no one wants to read a 50-page policy manual. The more concise and clear your policies are, the more likely people are to follow them. Use real-life examples and straight-forward rules that make sense. Policies are like traffic laws, they keep everyone moving safely in the same direction, even if they're driving different vehicles.

CYBERSECURITY TRAINING FOR SOLOPRENEURS

You might think that cybersecurity training is only necessary for big teams, but that's a dangerous assumption. Even if you're flying solo, keeping your skills sharp is one of the best investments you can make in your long-term business health. Threats evolve constantly, and staying up to date is the only way to stay ahead.

Start by learning how to recognize the most common cyber threats. Phishing emails and text messages are designed to trick you into giving up sensitive information. They often contain urgent messages, odd-looking links, or typos. Social engineering is a broader tactic where scammers manipulate your trust, such as pretending to be a vendor or client to gain access to information or systems. Then there's ransomware, a type of malware that locks your files and demands payment to unlock them. The best way to prevent this is by backing up your data regularly and keeping your software up to date.

So where can you learn? Great free resources are available through trusted organizations like NIST, CISA, and the Federal Trade Commission. These sites offer checklists, training guides, and alerts about new threats. If you prefer a more visual approach, YouTube channels and webinars from cybersecurity professionals can help you stay sharp. And don't forget to test yourself with free phishing simulations to see how well you can spot scams.

If you do have a small team, even a part-time assistant or a few contractors, cybersecurity training becomes even more essential. Try sharing weekly threat alerts or scam examples during brief team check-ins. A five-minute reminder about best practices can go a long way. You can also enroll your team in affordable cybersecurity basics courses through platforms like Udemy or Coursera.

Low-cost tools can help reinforce this training. Phishing simulators like KnowBe4 send fake scam emails to test whether you or your team would fall for them. Newsletters from cybersecurity blogs or agencies can provide a steady stream of helpful tips. And if you want to make learning more engaging, gamified training tools like Cyber Escape Online add a fun, competitive edge to building skills.

Training is like sharpening your tools. Even the best knife dulls over time if you don't take care of it. The same goes for your cybersecurity skills. Regular training—whether formal or informal—keeps you and your team prepared, aware, and confident.

By prioritizing your cybersecurity culture, crafting policies that make sense, and committing to ongoing training, you're laying a strong foundation for a cyber-safe business. Remember, cybersecurity isn't a one-and-done fix. It's like staying healthy—you need ongoing habits, checkups, and adjustments. But every small step you take today helps protect your business, your data, and your customers tomorrow. Consistency beats complexity, and awareness beats panic every time.

IMPLEMENTING NIST CSF 2.0 STEP-BY-STEP

So, you've made it this far—you've learned why cybersecurity matters, explored the Core 4 Principles, and built a culture that prioritizes safety. Now, it's time to roll up your sleeves and bring it all together by implementing the NIST Cybersecurity Framework (CSF) 2.0. Think of this chapter as your personalized roadmap to getting things done.

The NIST CSF is designed to work for businesses of all shapes and sizes, from solopreneurs managing a single laptop to small teams handling sensitive client data. The framework's strength lies in its flexibility; you can tailor it to fit your business's needs and scale it as you grow.

WHY FOLLOW A FRAMEWORK LIKE NIST CSF?

Imagine you're planning a road trip to a destination you've never visited before. Would you set off without a map or GPS? Probably not. You'd want a reliable guide to help you navigate the terrain, avoid dead ends, and reach your destination safely. The NIST CSF is that guide, helping you navigate the complex world of cybersecurity with confidence.

There are several key reasons why this framework is considered the gold standard, especially for small businesses and solopreneurs. First, it's scalable and flexible. The NIST CSF isn't a one-size-fits-all solution; it's more like a LEGO set. You can build the exact security system your business needs without having to use every single piece. Whether you're running a one-person shop or managing a small team, the framework grows with you.

Next, it's recognized and trusted. Big names in business and government rely on the NIST CSF, which means it's already been vetted by the best. Aligning your business with this framework not only protects you but also boosts your credibility. Customers, partners, and even regulators know you're serious about cybersecurity when you follow NIST.

Another big benefit is that it helps with compliance. Many cybersecurity regulations, such as HIPAA (for healthcare), PCI DSS (for payment information), and GLBA (for financial data), align with NIST CSF principles. By adopting this framework, you're not just protecting your business; you're also checking key compliance boxes that could save you from hefty fines.

One of the most underrated strengths of the framework is that it's easy to understand. Let's be honest: cybersecurity frameworks often feel like they're written in another language. NIST CSF is refreshingly clear. It's divided into six straightforward functions—Govern, Identify, Protect,

Detect, Respond, and Recover—making it easy to focus on what matters most without getting lost in tech-speak.

And let's not forget that it's cost-effective. Most small businesses don't have unlimited budgets for cybersecurity. NIST CSF doesn't require fancy, expensive solutions. Instead, it helps you prioritize what's critical, so you're spending your resources where they'll have the most impact.

WHY NIST CSF IS PERFECT FOR SOLOPRENEURS AND SMALL BUSINESSES

For solopreneurs and small businesses, cybersecurity often feels overwhelming. The threats are real, but the resources can feel scarce. That's exactly where NIST CSF shines. It levels the playing field—you don't need an IT department to follow this framework. NIST CSF breaks cybersecurity down into manageable chunks that you can handle, even with limited technical know-how.

It also protects your reputation. Trust is everything in business, and following NIST CSF sends a powerful message to your customers: "Your data is safe with us."

And most importantly, it keeps you ahead of the curve. Cyber threats evolve, but so does NIST CSF. By adopting this framework, you're not just playing defense; you're staying ahead of emerging risks.

WHAT YOU'LL LEARN IN THE NEXT FEW CHAPTERS

In the next few chapters, we'll break down the NIST CSF into actionable steps you can take today. You'll learn how to govern and identify risks by setting the foundation with clear rules and knowing exactly what you're protecting. You'll also learn how to protect and detect, putting up defenses and staying vigilant against potential threats. Finally, we'll cover how to respond and recover, so you know how to act fast in a crisis and bounce back stronger than ever.

Each section will include simple, real-world examples, tools you can use, and pro tips to make implementation as painless as possible.

A PRACTICAL APPROACH FOR SOLOPRENEURS AND SMALL TEAMS

This isn't a one-size-fits-all guide; it's your guide. Whether you're a solopreneur juggling customer data or a small team managing remote workers, we'll show you how to implement the framework at your own pace. No IT degree required, and no giant budget necessary.

By the end of this book, you'll have more than just a checklist; you'll have a working cybersecurity plan tailored to your business. So, grab a cup of coffee (or something stronger if it's been one of those days), and let's get started!

GOVERN - SETTING THE RULES

For many solopreneurs and small business owners, cybersecurity often feels like a tangle of tech jargon and expensive solutions designed for corporations with IT departments bigger than your entire team. But here's the truth: cybersecurity starts with leadership—and if you own the business, that means you.

The Govern function in the NIST Cybersecurity Framework (CSF) 2.0 is all about making sure your business knows what it's protecting, why it's important, and how to keep it secure. Whether you're a solo financial consultant or a health coach running a small virtual team, governance helps you build a foundation that's strong, simple, and scalable.

UNDERSTANDING YOUR ORGANIZATIONAL CONTEXT

Before you can protect your business, you have to understand it. This might sound obvious, but when was the last time you sat down and really thought about your mission, your customer promises, and what data or services are essential to delivering them?

Governance starts by placing cybersecurity in the context of your goals. Are you committed to maintaining HIPAA compliance as a virtual therapist? Do your clients expect financial privacy under GLBA? What promises do you make in your contracts? These questions shape everything that follows in your cybersecurity program.

Also consider the people who matter: your clients, your vendors, your team (if you have one), and regulators. Each group has expectations about how you handle information. The better you understand those expectations, the better you can shape your cybersecurity efforts to meet them.

CRAFTING A RISK MANAGEMENT STRATEGY THAT FITS

Big businesses hire whole departments to analyze risk. You just need a clear plan that fits your business size and risk tolerance. This means asking yourself:

- What could go wrong?
- How likely is it?
- And how bad would it be if it did?

Let's say you store client tax documents in cloud storage. A breach here could mean identity theft, lost business, or even legal action. That's a high-risk area—so your strategy should prioritize strong access controls, encryption, and regular backups.

A solid risk management strategy doesn't just identify threats. It spells out your **risk tolerance**—what you're willing to accept—and your **risk appetite**—how aggressive or conservative you want to be when managing those risks. These decisions guide everything from which tools you invest in to which services you choose to outsource.

And don't keep this in your head. Write it down. A simple one-page strategy goes a long way when it comes to staying focused and communicating with clients, vendors, or future team members. Big companies have dedicated risk officers. You have a spreadsheet—and that's all you really need to get started. In fact, your **CS4B Risk Register** file includes a risk matrix that helps turn the idea of "risk" into something you can actually measure and manage. Download the file from this webpage:

https://www.cybersecurity4biz.com/the-small-business-owners-cybersecurity-guide

Why You Need a Risk Matrix

Let's be real: trying to protect *everything* equally is exhausting and unnecessary. The risk matrix helps you sort your cybersecurity risks by how likely they are to happen and how much damage they would cause if they did. This way, you can focus your limited time and resources on the stuff that really matters.

It's like sorting your to-do list. Some tasks are urgent and important (fix those first!), while others can wait. Your risk matrix is your cybersecurity to-do list.

How to Use the Risk Matrix in the CS4B Risk Register

Your spreadsheet is already structured to make this easy. Here's how to walk through it:

Step 1: Identify Risks

In the **"Risk Description"** column, write down potential threats to your business. Don't overthink it; just jot down what keeps you up at night. For example:

- "Client data stored in Google Drive could be accessed if my laptop is stolen."
- "Forgotten admin accounts on old platforms might still have access."
- "No formal process for updating plugins on my WordPress site."

If you're stuck, think through what would happen if someone got access to your email, your files, your website, or your client data.

Step 2: Assign Likelihood and Impact

Using the dropdown menus in the spreadsheet, assign each risk a:

- **Likelihood** (e.g., Rare, Unlikely, Possible, Likely, Almost Certain)
- **Impact** (e.g., Insignificant, Minor, Moderate, Major, Catastrophic)

Tip: Be honest, not optimistic. If you haven't updated your laptop in a year, a vulnerability exploit might be more "Likely" than you'd like to admit.

Step 3: Calculate Risk Level

The spreadsheet will automatically assign a **risk level** (Low, Medium, High, or Extreme) based on where that risk falls on the matrix. This visualizes your priorities clearly, so you can tackle the big stuff first.

Think of it like color-coding your risk:

- ⬤ **Low** = Monitor, but don't lose sleep.
- ◯ **Medium** = Fix soon.
- ⬤ **High** = Fix now.
- ⬤ **Extreme** = This is the cyber equivalent of a fire alarm. Address it *yesterday.*

Step 4: Document Mitigation Actions

In the **"Mitigation"** column, write out what you're going to do (or already do) to reduce that risk. For example:

- Enable two-factor authentication.
- Remove unused user accounts.
- Set a reminder to run updates monthly.

This keeps you accountable and gives you a record to show clients, auditors, or just your future self when you revisit the list.

Step 5: Review and Update Regularly

Risks change. Maybe you switched to a more secure email provider. Maybe a new threat popped up (looking at you, AI voice scams). Set a reminder—quarterly is great—to revisit your risk register and update it.

This also makes you look incredibly put-together when a client asks, "What are you doing about cybersecurity?" and you can say, "Funny you should ask. I've got a risk register."

A Living Document, Not a One-and-Done

Your risk register isn't meant to be perfect; it's meant to be useful. As your business grows, you'll get better at identifying risks, quicker at evaluating them, and more strategic about how you respond.

The beauty of using a simple spreadsheet is that it's yours. You can tweak the categories, add a "Last Reviewed" date, color-code your tasks—whatever works for your brain and your workflow.

Just like bookkeeping or meal prepping, risk management becomes easier the more you do it. And it's one of the most empowering things you can do as a business owner: to know what threats exist and exactly how you're keeping them in check.

DEFINING ROLES, RESPONSIBILITIES, AND ACCOUNTABILITY

Even if you're a one-person powerhouse, defining roles is still critical. Why? Because it creates clarity. You might be doing everything, but breaking tasks into roles (like "cyber hygiene," "software management," or "data access reviews") makes it easier to build habits and eventually hand off responsibilities as you grow.

If you work with freelancers, a virtual assistant, or an IT contractor, it's essential that they understand their role in protecting your data. Governance means creating a simple "who does what" cheat sheet for cybersecurity—who has access to what systems, who updates software, who handles customer data, and who's in charge if something goes wrong.

If something falls through the cracks, you want to know who's responsible—not who's to blame, but who is empowered to take action.

DEVELOPING AND MAINTAINING CYBERSECURITY POLICIES

Policies don't have to be 50-page documents full of legalese. In fact, short and clear is better. Think of your cybersecurity policies as your business's user manual for safe operations.

A few key areas to cover:

- **Acceptable use** – How are work devices, information, and accounts to be used?
- **Password management** – Are you using a password manager? How often do passwords get changed?
- **Access control** – How do you ensure that only authorized users can see sensitive information?
- **Data protection** – What data do you collect and how is it stored, accessed, and shared?
- **Cybersecurity plan** – How do you protect your devices and data?
- **Incident response** – What's your first move if something goes wrong?
- **Data breach plan** – What's your plan if you have a breach? How do you notify those affected?

Review these policies regularly. Once a year is a good start. Anytime you add a new tool, change a workflow, or expand your team, give your policies a quick tune-up.

KEEPING AN EYE ON THE BIG PICTURE (OVERSIGHT)

Governance doesn't stop once you've written some policies and set your roles. It's an ongoing process that should evolve as your business grows or as new threats emerge.

Oversight means checking in regularly to see what's working and what isn't. Maybe your risk tolerance has changed, or maybe a new regulation affects your industry. Governance gives you the structure to adjust without having to start from scratch each time.

This doesn't have to be fancy. A quarterly cybersecurity check-in—just you and your coffee—is a great way to stay ahead. Ask yourself:

- Have I reviewed access permissions recently?
- Are my backups working?
- Did I install the latest software updates?
- Do I still feel confident about how I'm handling sensitive information?

These check-ins ensure your risk management strategy stays alive—not buried in a dusty file folder.

MANAGING YOUR CYBERSECURITY SUPPLY CHAIN

In today's connected world, you probably use third-party services—cloud storage, scheduling tools, invoicing platforms, maybe even a web developer. Each of these creates a link in your cybersecurity chain.

Governance means evaluating those links and making sure they're strong. It's your responsibility to ask:

- How do my vendors protect my data?
- Do they have a track record of keeping customer info secure?
- What happens if they go offline or get breached?

This doesn't mean ditching every tool that isn't bulletproof, but it does mean having a plan. Review contracts, set up multi-factor authentication on all accounts, and don't give more access than necessary. If your virtual assistant doesn't need your banking login, don't share it.

WHY GOVERNANCE IS THE SECRET WEAPON OF CYBER RESILIENCE

The Govern function is like the frame of a house—it holds everything else together. Without it, even the best tools and tech solutions can fall apart. But with it? You've got a structure that supports everything from compliance to customer trust.

Here's what governance really gives you:

- **Alignment** – Your cybersecurity efforts support your goals, not distract from them.
- **Accountability** – Everyone (even just you) knows what to do and when to do it.

- **Communication** – You can talk about your cybersecurity strategy with clients, partners, or auditors with confidence.
- **Compliance** – You stay ahead of rules and regulations, not scrambling to catch up.
- **Resilience** – You bounce back faster when something goes wrong because you have a plan.

FINAL THOUGHTS: YOU'RE ALREADY THE BOSS— NOW BE THE CISO

You don't need a huge budget, a giant team, or a tech degree to lead your business toward better cybersecurity. You just need clarity, intention, and a willingness to set the rules.

The Govern function isn't about being perfect. It's about knowing what matters, putting guardrails in place, and adjusting as you grow.

And remember good governance isn't about being scared of what could go wrong, it's about being ready, confident, and in control when something does.

IDENTIFY - UNDERSTANDING WHAT'S AT RISK

Before you can protect your business, you need to understand what you're protecting. That's the essence of the **Identify** function in NIST CSF—it's about creating a clear picture of your digital assets, vulnerabilities, and risks. Think of it as taking inventory before you build a fortress: you can't secure what you don't know exists.

This chapter will guide you through:

1. Mapping your assets to identify what you have to protect.
2. Conducting a simple risk assessment to understand your vulnerabilities.
3. Breaking down compliance requirements so you know what's expected of you.

1. Mapping Your Assets: What Do You Have to Protect?

The first step in identifying your risks is knowing what's at stake. This means taking a detailed inventory of everything that could be targeted in a cyberattack. These are your **assets**, and they fall into a few key categories:

- **Data**
- **Hardware**
- **Software**
- **People**
- **Compliance Requirements**
- **Risk Assessment**

Let's go over each area now.

DATA CLASSIFICATION

Create a Data Flow Document to track who uses what and why. Not every employee needs access to all of your information. Your marketing staff shouldn't need or be allowed to view employee payroll data, and your administrative staff may not need access to all your customer information.

When you inventory your data and know exactly what data you have and where it's kept, it is important to assign access rights to that data. Doing so simply means creating a list of the specific employees, partners, or contractors who have access to specific data under what circumstances, and how those access privileges will be managed and tracked.

Your business could have a variety of data of varying value, including:

A. Contact Information

- First & Last Name Combination
- E-mail addresses
- Phone numbers
- Mailing Address

B. Personal Identification

- Social Security number
- Date of Birth
- Driver's license number or state-issued identification card number
- Employment data

C. Income Information

- Income data
- Tax filing data
- Retirement plan data
- Asset ownership data
- Investment data
- Previous tax returns

D. Financial information:

- Financial account number
- Credit or debit card number with or without Card Verification Value (CVV) and expiration date.
- Access codes, personal identification number, or password(s) that permit access to a client's financial accounts

E. Database Information

- Purchase history
- CRM data
- Tax prep software data
- Financial statements

WHAT IS A DATA FLOW MAP & WHY DOES IT MATTER?

A **data flow map** shows how information moves through your business. Think of it like Google Maps for your customer's data. It answers questions like:

- Where does info come from?
- Who touches it?
- Where does it go?
- Where does it rest?

Creating a map of this journey helps you identify security gaps, meet compliance requirements (like **NIST CSF**,

HIPAA, **GLBA**, etc.), and be prepared if something goes wrong.

Now let's fill out the data flow spreadsheet you can download from here:

https://www.cybersecurity4biz.com/the-small-business-owners-cybersecurity-guide

Your spreadsheet is built around tracking how different types of information move step-by-step through your systems and people. Row 3 is your header row, and each row after that is one "data journey."

Before You Start:

Make a list of the types of data you collect and handle, such as:

- Contact info
- Health info
- Payment info
- Login credentials

Now follow the flow...

1. Type of Information

What to put: The category of information.

✎ Examples:

- Contact Information
- Health Information (PHI)
- Financial Information
- Personal Identification (SSN, DOB, Driver's License)

This helps with risk classification later.

2. Who Requests the Information

What to put: The person, software, or process that collects the info from the customer.

✎ Examples:

- Website form
- John Doe via phone
- Online booking form
- Intake specialist

3. Who Inputs the Information

What to put: The person or system that actually enters the data into your tools.

Examples:

- Customer enters into Google Form
- Employee enters into Monday.com
- Auto-import from email

4. Who It Gets Passed to Next

What to put: Where the data goes after it's entered.

Examples:

- CRM sends to MailChimp
- Google Form to Google Sheet
- Accounting tool (like QuickBooks)

This is where you track integrations or human handoffs.

5. Where the Data Is Stored

What to put: The final destination(s) where the information is kept.

Examples:

- Cloud (e.g., Google Drive, Dropbox, CRM)
- Local computer
- Paper filing cabinet
- Encrypted USB

6. *(Optional Column)* Notes or Observations

Use the extra columns for red flags, planned improvements, or clarifying comments.

✎ Examples:

- "Needs MFA added"
- "Stored unencrypted—fix this!"
- "Auto-deletes after 90 days"

Once you've identified your data, keep a record of its location and move it to more appropriate locations as needed. Start by making folders for each type of data, i.e., public, internal, confidential, and regulated. Each individual file should be labeled as to the type of data it contains as well. For example, the word "internal" should be in the name of all policy files.

Categorization

Categorize your data into four types (Public, Internal, Confidential, Regulated).

Public

- Public Data that may be disclosed to any person, regardless of affiliation with your business. Some level of control is required to protect the integrity and availability of Public data (e.g., protecting original (source) documents from unauthorized modification). Examples are public-facing web pages, directory data (e.g., contact information), press releases, maps, newsletters, newspapers and magazines.

Internal

- Internal Data not intended for public use or exposure. Internal data generally should not be disclosed outside of the company without the permission of the person or group that created the data. Any data not specifically classified as Regulated, Confidential, or Public should be considered Internal. Examples are Proprietary business information, produced for use only by your organization members (e.g., Employee ID numbers), Internal operating procedures and operational manuals, Internal memoranda, emails, reports and other documents, Contact lists that contain information that is not publicly available, Technical documents, Business Process information.

Confidential

- Confidential Data protected as Confidential by contracts, or third-party agreement or otherwise designated by the organization for confidential treatment. Unauthorized disclosure, alteration, or destruction of this data type could cause a significant level of risk to the Business or its affiliates. Examples are job applications, client files, employee files, Intellectual Property, Business Processes, Employee Handbooks, research data, data protected by confidentiality agreements Law enforcement, court records and confidential investigation records, Citizen or immigration status, Detailed information about the organizations buildings, activities or events, including facility security system details.

Regulated

- Regulated Data protected or controlled by federal, state, local, and/or industry laws or regulations. These data are affected by data breach notification laws and contractual provisions in government, which impose legal and technical restrictions on the appropriate use of the information. Examples are:

o Personally Identifiable Information (PII) which is any information about an individual maintained by an agency, including (1) any information that can be used to distinguish or trace an individual's identity, such as name, social security number, date and place of birth, mother's maiden name, or biometric records; and (2) any other information that is linked or linkable to an individual, such as medical, educational, financial, and employment information. This includes but not limited to Social Security Numbers, Credit Card Numbers, Financial/ Banking Account Numbers, Driver's License Numbers, Health Insurance Policy ID Numbers.

o The Health Insurance Portability and Accountability Act (HIPAA) establishes national standards to protect individuals' medical records and other personal health information and applies to health plans, health care clearinghouses, and those health care providers that conduct certain health care transactions electronically. The rules require appropriate safeguards to protect the privacy of personal health information and set limits and conditions on the uses and disclosures that may be made of such information without patient authorization. The rules also give patients' rights over their health information, including rights to examine and obtain a copy of their health records, and to request corrections.

o The Gramm-Leach-Bliley Act (GLBA) protects consumers' nonpublic personal information (NPI) that is collected by financial institutions. This includes financial information like account numbers, bank balances, loan or payment history, credit or debit card information, income details, and credit scores. In addition, GLBA protects information related to transactions or services that a consumer engages in with a financial institution. This includes data provided to obtain a financial product or service, information resulting from transactions, and any data obtained in the course of providing services, such as credit reports. Even information derived internally—like risk profiles or credit ratings generated by the institution—is protected.

Data shall have controlled access according to the table below for details.

	Access	Transmission	Email	Storage
Public	Open	Open	Open	Open
Internal	Limited	Open	Open	Open
Confidential	Need-to-know	Encrypted	Encrypted	Encrypted
Regulated	Regulated by law	Encrypted	Encrypted	Encrypted

Create Your Folders

Start by making folders for each type of data: public, internal, confidential, and regulated. If you have whole disk encryption you are able to store them all in one place, if not, create a partition or folder and encrypt it. The "Public" and "Internal" folders can be stored in the unencrypted partition. However, you need to place the "Confidential" and "Restricted" folders in the encrypted partition.

I know this sounds a little painful; however, separating your data into four folders on two separate partitions will be much more secure. If a cyberattack occurs, they will not get all your data at once. It also gives you a way to control access to the folders You can assign users access to the folders based on what level of sensitive information they need to complete their jobs. This is otherwise known as the "minimum necessary" rule, giving them the minimum necessary access to information that they need to do the job.

Label Your Files

Each individual file should be labeled in the header as internal, confidential, or regulated. This ensures that anyone seeing the document will know its contents contain classified information. Examples are shown below:

Internal Use Only
Confidential
HIPPA Regulated

HARDWARE

Document all the hardware your organization uses (even if it's owned by the employees or contractors). Include make/model, owner's name, who is using it, dates put into service, and as many technical specs as possible.

- Laptops, desktops, tablets, and smartphones.
  - Servers, routers, and network equipment.
  - External storage devices like USB drives or external hard drives.

Now let's gather a list of your hardware and add it to the spreadsheet you can download from here:

https://www.cybersecurity4biz.com/the-small-business-owners-cybersecurity-guide

Fill it out by adding your information to the rows.

1. Hardware Item

What to put: What type of device is it?

Examples: Work Laptop, Office Printer, WiFi Router, Mobile Phone

2. Location

What to put: Where this device lives.

Examples: Home Office, Main Office, Front Desk, Storage Closet

This matters in case of loss, theft, or support needs—especially if you're hybrid or remote!

3. Manufacturer / Model

What to put: Brand and model number.

Examples: Dell Latitude 7650, HP LaserJet M404, Netgear Nighthawk AC1900

4. Principal User

What to put: Name of the person who uses it most.

Examples: Jane Doe, Todd Mitchell, Shared

5. In-Service Date

What to put: Date the device was first used.

Example: 2024-02-28

Helps track when devices are due for updates or retirement (tech ages faster than milk).

6. Computer Device Name

What to put: The internal or visible name of the computer on your network.

✎ *Examples:* BB-Jane, Office-Printer1, Router-GuestNet

This can help your IT support or security person track things down quickly.

7. Operating System

What to put: The software platform the device runs on.

✎ *Examples:* Windows 11 Pro, iOS 17, Android 14, macOS Sonoma

8. RAM

What to put: How much memory the device has.

✎ *Examples:* 8 GB, 16 GB, 64 MB (if it's vintage)

9. Hard Drive Size

What to put: Storage capacity.

✎ *Examples:* 256 GB SSD, 1 TB HDD

10. Processor

What to put: The CPU type inside the device.

✎ *Examples:* Intel i7, M2 Pro, AMD Ryzen 5, Intel 3705

✅ **Pro Tips for Small Business Owners:**

- **Don't guess—check your device settings or right-click "This PC" (on Windows) or "About This Mac."**
- **Use this for insurance records and warranty claims, too.**

- **Review and update this list quarterly or when you buy or retire a device.**
- **Store this file securely**—in an encrypted folder, cloud drive with MFA, or password-protected spreadsheet.

SOFTWARE AND SYSTEMS

Document all the software your organization uses (downloaded, cloud, and SaaS you are using). Include the function it serves, the owner's name, who is using it, dates put into service, and as many technical specs as possible.

- Email platforms, accounting software, and CRMs.
  - Cloud services, such as Google Workspace or Microsoft 365.
  - Your website and any associated apps.

Now, let's gather a list of your software and add it to the spreadsheet you can download from here:

https://www.cybersecurity4biz.com/the-small-business-owners-cybersecurity-guide

Fill it out by adding your information to the rows.

1. Software Item

What to put: Name and version of the software or app.

🔧 *Examples:* QuickBooks 2023, Microsoft 365, Zoom, Adobe Acrobat Pro, Bitdefender Antivirus

Include everything you use to do business—even free tools or browser-based platforms.

2. Function

What to put: What is this software used for?

🔧 *Examples:* Accounting, Communication, Document Signing, Marketing, Project Management

Ask: "What job does this software do for me?"

3. Principal User

What to put: Who primarily uses this software?

🔧 *Examples:* Jane Doe, Todd Mitchell, Everyone

If it's company-wide, you can say "All Staff."

4. Location of Software Media/Disks

What to put: Where is the install file or license key stored?

🔧 *Examples:* Online, Encrypted USB, Cloud Account, File Server

If it's cloud-based, just write "Online"—no need to go hunting for floppy disks.

5. Location of Data

What to put: Where does the data live that this software creates or manages?

✎ *Examples:* Local Drive, Cloud (Google Drive, iCloud), NAS, External Hard Drive

Cloud storage needs to be secured just like local devices.

6. Is Software Critical to Operations (Yes/No)?

What to put: Would business grind to a halt if this software failed?

✎ *Examples:* Yes (for QuickBooks), No (for Canva), Yes (for HIPAA EMR)

This helps you prioritize backups, updates, and licensing.

☑ **Quick Pro Tips:**

- **Include your antivirus, VPN, and any password manager.**
- **Update this list every 6 months** or when adding/removing tools.
- **Tie software to your hardware.** If Jane's laptop has QuickBooks, it should be in both inventories.

PEOPLE

Document all the people in your organization, including the third-party services your organization uses (your supply chain, contractors, office management, payroll, etc.). Include the access level they have to data, the function they serve, contact info, who is using it, dates put into service, and as many technical specs as possible.

- All employees
  - Payment processors like PayPal or Stripe.
  - Vendors who have access to your systems or data (bookkeepers, marketing agencies, virtual assistants, etc.).

Pro Tip: Use a simple spreadsheet or checklist to track your assets. Note what each item is, where it's located, who uses it, and how critical it is to your operations.

Analogy Time: Mapping your assets is like creating a treasure map of your business. If you don't know where the treasure is, how will you keep the pirates out?

Why This Is Important

You rely on outside help—insurance agents, legal pros, financial advisors—to keep your business running and protected. But in a crisis, can you find their number, policy, or contract? NIST CSF encourages documenting these relationships because:

- If something goes wrong (like a breach or lawsuit), you'll know who to call.
- It supports **supply chain risk management**.
- You can align policies and responsibilities more easily.

Now let's gather a list of your other third-party assets and add it to the spreadsheet you can download from here:

https://www.cybersecurity4biz.com/the-small-business-owners-cybersecurity-guide

Fill it out by adding your information to the rows.

1. Company/Broker

What to put: The name of the insurance provider, broker, or agency.

🔧 *Examples:* State Farm, LegalZoom Insurance, Cybersecurity4biz LLC

2. Company/Broker Tel. Nbr.

What to put: The phone number for your contact at the company.

🔧 *Examples:* (800) 555-1234, (555) 555-1234

Bonus points if you include your agent's name in parentheses.

3. Company/Broker Address

What to put: Mailing or physical address of the provider.

Examples: 123 Main St., Albuquerque, NM 87101

4. Policy Number

What to put: The number listed on your insurance policy.

Examples: CYB-2023-44567, BIZGEN-0001234

Needed for claims, renewals, and proving you're covered.

5. Type of Policy

What to put: What kind of coverage it is.

Examples: General Liability, Cyber Insurance, Professional Liability, Errors & Omissions

6. What's Covered?

What to put: Short summary of what the policy includes.

Examples: "Data breaches, ransomware, client lawsuits," or "Property damage, bodily injury"

This helps quickly assess gaps in your coverage.

7. Location of Documents

What to put: Where you keep the full policy document.

Examples: Google Drive > Insurance Folder, Locked Filing Cabinet, Encrypted USB

Don't just leave this on your desk or floating in your inbox.

WHO HAS ACCESS?

An **Access List** is like the guest list to your digital house party —you need to know who's coming in, what rooms they're allowed in, and when they leave. In cybersecurity, this helps you enforce **"least privilege"** (only giving people access to what they truly need) and proves that you're taking proactive steps to control sensitive information. It's not just good practice; it's required by most compliance frameworks such as **HIPAA, GLBA, and NIST CSF.**

Now let's gather a list of access to sensitive information you have granted to employees, contractors, third-party vendors, interns, etc., and add it to the spreadsheet you can download from here:

https://www.cybersecurity4biz.com/the-small-business-owners-cybersecurity-guide

How to Fill Out Your Access List Spreadsheet

1. Name

What to put: The employee or contractor's full name.

✎ Example: Jane Doe, John Smith

2. Role

What to put: Their job title or function in your business.

🔧 Example: Owner, Virtual Assistant, Intern, Billing Specialist

3. Job Duties

What to put: A short summary of what they do.

🔧 Example: Scheduling, Accounting, Marketing, Customer Service

Helps you justify their access level.

4. Access Level

What to put: What kind of access they have to sensitive data.

🔧 Examples:

- Full access to all PII
- Billing system only
- Contact info only
- Admin dashboard access

Make this as specific as possible—it shows you're managing risk.

5. Date Access Granted

What to put: The day they were given access.

🔧 Example: 2024-06-14

6. Date Access Terminated

What to put: The date access was removed (if they left or changed roles).

🔧 Example: 2024-07-01

Always remove access when someone leaves. Don't ghost on offboarding!

☑️ **Pro Tips:**

- **Review this list quarterly.** People come and go, and roles change.
- **Use this to prep for audits or breach investigations.**
- **Tie it to system logs or permissions when possible.**

COMPLIANCE REQUIREMENTS (IN PLAIN ENGLISH)

Cybersecurity isn't just a good idea—it's often the law. Depending on your industry and location, you may be required to follow specific regulations to protect sensitive data. Here's a breakdown of common compliance requirements:

- **HIPAA (Health Insurance Portability and Accountability Act):**

  If you handle patient health information, you're

required to secure it against breaches and unauthorized access.

- **PCI DSS (Payment Card Industry Data Security Standard):**

Businesses that process credit card payments must meet these standards to prevent fraud and data theft.

- **GLBA (Gramm-Leach-Bliley Act):**

Financial institutions, including bookkeepers and tax preparers, must protect customer financial data.

- **CMMC (Cybersecurity Maturity Model Certification):**

Government contractors and sub-contractors must meet strict cybersecurity and privacy regulations to obtain and retain contracts.

- **GDPR (General Data Protection Regulation):**

If you do business with customers in the EU, you're responsible for protecting their personal data and being transparent about how you use it.

- **Various State Consumer Privacy Laws:**

Similar to GDPR but focused on state residents, these

laws give consumers more control over their personal information.

- **Industry Standards**:

  In some cases, you'll need to meet specific requirements set by your industry or professional organizations.

Pro Tip: Compliance isn't just about avoiding fines—it's a way to show customers you take their privacy seriously. Use it as a selling point in your marketing!

Analogy Time: Think of compliance as the rules of the road. You could ignore stop signs and speed limits, but the consequences can be costly—and potentially disastrous.

CONDUCTING A RISK ASSESSMENT (WITHOUT OVERCOMPLICATING IT)

Now that you know what you're protecting, it's time to figure out where you're vulnerable. The risk assessment you completed in the last chapter helps you prioritize your efforts by focusing on the most likely and impactful threats. You may want to revisit that list and make any changes now that you have identified all your assets in writing.

Here's a review from the last chapter where we discussed Risk Management:

- **Step 1: Identify Threats**
  - What could go wrong? Examples include

phishing attacks, malware infections, or accidental data leaks.

- **Step 2: Assess Vulnerabilities**
  - Where are you exposed? For example:
    - Weak passwords.
    - Outdated software.
    - Employees are unaware of phishing scams.
- **Step 3: Evaluate Impact**
  - If a threat exploited a vulnerability, how bad would it be? Consider:
    - Financial loss.
    - Reputational damage.
    - Legal or regulatory consequences.
- **Step 4: Prioritize Risks**
  - Focus on high-impact, high-likelihood risks first. For instance, if your employees routinely receive phishing emails, training them to spot these threats should be a top priority.

Analogy Time: Think of a risk assessment like checking your car before a road trip. If your brakes are squealing, you'd fix those before worrying about a slightly dirty windshield. Focus on what's critical first.

Why Identifying Risks is Critical

By mapping your assets, assessing risks, and understanding your compliance obligations, you're laying the groundwork for a strong cybersecurity strategy. You can't protect what you don't know about, and you can't fix vulnerabilities you haven't identified.

With this clear picture in place, you're ready to move on to the next step in the NIST CSF framework: **Protect**—putting up defenses to keep threats out. Let's dive into that next!

PROTECT - SAFEGUARDING YOUR BUSINESS

Protecting your business is like securing a fortress: it requires strong locks, vigilant guards, and a plan for every possible entry point. This chapter will guide you through essential tools and strategies to safeguard your operations, ensuring you're prepared to repel threats before they can cause harm.

We'll focus on six critical areas:

1. **Access Control and Password Security**
2. **Data Encryption and Secure Storage**
3. **Software Updates and Patch Management**
4. **Recognizing and Preventing Social Engineering**
5. **Protecting Your Identity and Devices**
6. **Facility Security**

ACCESS CONTROL AND PASSWORD SECURITY

Access control and password security are foundational because they dictate who can access your business's systems and sensitive data. Without them, you leave the doors to your digital fortress wide open, allowing bad actors to walk in unchallenged. Strong access policies and secure passwords ensure that only the right people get in, and they help prevent both internal mistakes and external breaches.

Access control is the backbone of cybersecurity—it ensures that the right people have access to the right resources at the right time. Paired with strong password security, it becomes a powerful barrier against unauthorized access.

Access Control Best Practices

- **Role-Based Access Control (RBAC):** Assign permissions based on job responsibilities, ensuring that employees only access data necessary for their tasks.
  - Example: Bookkeepers access financial records; marketing contractors access social media tools.
  - Scenario: A small accounting firm uses RBAC to ensure that junior staff can view client data but cannot edit it, while senior staff have editing privileges for tax filing.
- **Principle of Least Privilege:** Only grant access to what's absolutely necessary. Avoid "admin rights" unless required.
- **Access Control Lists:** Regularly update and audit access control lists to ensure permissions align with current job roles.
  - Example: A solopreneur reviews their CRM system monthly to ensure that external

consultants no longer have access after completing projects.

- **Logging Off Devices:** Employees must log off or lock their devices when unattended. Implement automatic timeouts to log users off after inactivity.
  - Example: A small design agency configures laptops to lock after five minutes of inactivity to protect client design drafts.
- **Secure Offboarding:** Collect access cards, keys, and IT equipment from employees on or before their last day of employment. Disable their accounts immediately.
  - Scenario: A boutique retailer terminates a staff member and immediately disables their access to the inventory and sales systems to prevent unauthorized activity.

Password Security Best Practices

- Ban weak passwords such as "123456" or "password."
- Require strong passwords with at least fourteen characters, including a mix of uppercase, lowercase, numbers, and symbols. Use passphrases, e.g., "Tim3F*rV@cati0n."
- Enforce unique passwords for every work account and recommend using a password manager.
- Implement Multi-Factor Authentication (MFA):
  - Combine something you know (password), something you have (a hardware token or phone), and something you are (biometric data).

- Use authentication apps (e.g., Google Authenticator) or hardware tokens for higher security.
- Eliminate routine password expiration policies unless there's evidence of compromise. Reset passwords immediately if compromised.

Advanced Technologies for Access Control

- **Biometric Authentication:** Use fingerprint or facial recognition for sensitive systems.
  - Example: A health clinic uses fingerprint scanners to restrict access to patient health records to authorized staff only.
- **Zero Trust Architecture:** Continuously verify users and devices before granting access.
  - Scenario: A remote-first tech startup uses a zero-trust platform to verify both the identity and location of employees accessing the company database.

Access control is the backbone of cybersecurity—it ensures that the right people have access to the right resources at the right time. Paired with strong password security, it becomes a powerful barrier against unauthorized access.

DATA ENCRYPTION AND SECURE STORAGE

Data encryption and secure storage ensure that even if a hacker or unauthorized individual gains access to your files, the information remains unreadable without the proper decryption key. This layer of protection not only shields your sensitive data from prying eyes but also demonstrates compliance with regulations such as HIPAA, PCI-DSS, and GLBA, which mandate encryption for sensitive information. Using these tools sends a clear message to your customers: "Your data is safe with us."

Encryption turns sensitive information into unreadable code, ensuring only authorized individuals can access it. It's essential for protecting data at rest and in transit.

Encryption Best Practices

- **Full-Disk Encryption:** Use tools like BitLocker (Windows) or FileVault (macOS) to secure all data on devices.
- Common email does not use end-to-end encryption. Use secure email services like ProtonMail or third-party software for sensitive messages.
- **End-to-End Encryption for Cloud Services:** Select platforms that offer robust encryption.

Secure Storage Practices

- Use encrypted external drives for offline backups, storing them in a locked, secure location.
- Ensure cloud backups use encryption and multi-factor authentication.
- **File Versioning:** Track changes by saving new versions of files, using a naming convention like "file_v1," "file_v2," etc.

- **Checksums:** Verify file integrity by comparing hash values between original and copied files.

Why Encryption Matters

Encryption is often a compliance requirement for businesses handling financial, healthcare, or personal data under regulations such as HIPAA, PCI-DSS, or GLBA.

SOFTWARE UPDATES AND PATCH MANAGEMENT

Keeping software up to date is like sealing cracks in your home before a storm hits—it prevents vulnerabilities from being exploited. Outdated software often has known flaws that attackers can exploit to gain access to your systems. By implementing regular updates and proactive patch management, you stay ahead of cybercriminals and ensure the integrity of your business systems. This also helps meet compliance requirements for standards like PCI-DSS and CMMC, which emphasize maintaining secure software environments.

Unpatched software is a common vulnerability exploited by cybercriminals. Regular updates and patch management are critical to minimizing risks.

Steps for Effective Patch Management

1. **Automate Updates:** Enable automatic updates for operating systems, browsers, antivirus software, and other critical applications. Tools can streamline this process for solopreneurs and small teams.

2. **Maintain an Inventory of Software:** Keep a detailed list of software and plugins to track update requirements. Use platforms for easier software tracking.

3. **Monitor Vulnerability Alerts:** Subscribe to notifications from vendors or organizations like the Cybersecurity and Infrastructure Security Agency (CISA).

4. **Test Updates:** For critical systems, test patches in a controlled environment to prevent disruptions. Virtual Machine software can help create testing environments.

5. **Replace Unsupported Software:** Outdated software without vendor support is a huge risk. Replace it immediately.

Additional Protections

- Configure email applications to prevent automatic image loading, reducing the risk of malware.
- Use Microsoft Office "Protected View" to open attachments in read-only mode by default.
- Set up spam filters and educate users to recognize phishing attempts.

By leveraging tools, small businesses can ensure consistent patch management and reduce their exposure to cyber threats.

RECOGNIZING AND PREVENTING SOCIAL ENGINEERING

Social engineering is a hacker's favorite tool because it targets human vulnerabilities rather than technical weaknesses. People are often the weakest link in cybersecurity, making education and vigilance critical. Recognizing and preventing social engineering attacks not only helps safeguard your business from breaches but also builds a culture of awareness and accountability within your organization.

Hackers use manipulation, deception, and urgency to trick victims into providing sensitive information or access.

Common Social Engineering Tactics

- **Phishing:** Fraudulent emails, texts, or calls impersonating trusted entities.
    - Real-World Example: You receive an email claiming to be from your bank, urging you to "verify your account due to unusual activity." The email includes a link to a fake login page designed to steal your credentials.
    - Screenshot Idea: Consider including a screenshot of a phishing email highlighting red flags like spelling errors, suspicious URLs, and urgent language to help readers recognize common tactics.
    - Example: An email pretending to be your bank asks you to "verify your account."
- **Pretexting:** Creating a fake scenario to manipulate victims, such as posing as IT support.

- **Baiting:** Offering something enticing, like free software, to trick users into downloading malware.

Red Flags to Watch For

- Messages with urgent demands, e.g., "Act now or lose access!"
- Unfamiliar senders or domains with minor misspellings (e.g., "amaz0n.com").
- Requests for sensitive information via email or text.

Defensive Strategies

1. **Verify Requests Independently:** Contact the company directly using official channels.
2. **Hover Before You Click:** Check links for suspicious URLs.
3. **Train Regularly:** Use phishing simulations and ongoing education.
4. **Enable MFA:** Even if credentials are compromised, MFA can block unauthorized access.

PROTECTING YOUR IDENTITY AND DEVICES

Protecting your identity and devices goes beyond securing your network; it's about maintaining your credibility and operational integrity. Hackers often target individuals as an entry point to compromise a broader system. By safeguarding your personal and professional digital identities, you reduce the risk of unauthorized access, identity theft, and reputational damage. Securing devices also ensures that the tools you rely on to run your business remain operational and trustworthy.

Identity Protection Tips

- **Browse Anonymously:** Use VPNs or proxy servers to mask your location and activity.
- **Use Junk Email Accounts:** Create separate email accounts for non-critical purposes.
- **Encrypted Messaging Apps:** Use apps that offer encryption for private communication.

Device Protection Tips

- Secure Internet of Things devices, such as Nest, Ring, Alexa, and smart appliances, by isolating them on a guest network.
- Dispose of electronic equipment securely, ensuring all data is wiped or hard drives are shredded.
- Lock external media (e.g., USB drives, CDs) when not in use to prevent theft or unauthorized access.

Security Setup Checklist for New Devices (Computer, Tablet, or Phone)

Install Updates Immediately & Enable Auto-Updates

- Keep the operating system, software, and apps current.
- Many breaches exploit outdated systems; updates fix these vulnerabilities quickly.

Use Strong Passwords and a Password Manager

- Create unique, complex passwords (longer is stronger!).
- Use a password manager to avoid repeat passwords or sticky notes.

Enable Multi-Factor Authentication (MFA)

- Add a second layer of protection to all critical accounts.
- Prefer **authenticator apps** or **hardware keys** over text verification.

Enable Device Encryption

- Encrypt your device to protect data if it's lost or stolen.
- Turn on:
  - **BitLocker** for Windows
  - **FileVault** for macOS
  - **iOS and Android** encryption (usually on by default—verify in settings)

Turn On Built-in Firewalls

- Firewalls help block unauthorized access.
- Make sure they're enabled on computers and routers.

Install Reputable Antivirus or Mobile Security Tools

- For Windows/macOS: install well-rated antivirus/malware protection.
- For Android/iOS: consider mobile security apps

Review and Limit App Permissions

- Apps often ask for way more access than they need.
- Disable access to the camera, microphone, contacts, etc., if not essential.

Disable Wireless Features When Not in Use

- Bluetooth, Wi-Fi, NFC, and location services are data leaks waiting to happen.
- Turn them off when not actively using them, especially in public.

Backup Your Data Securely

- Use encrypted backups:
  - Local (external hard drive)
  - Cloud (from a trusted provider with strong security settings)

Remove Unnecessary Apps and Bloatware

- Unused or pre-installed apps can be security risks.
- Only keep what's necessary and trusted.

EASM TOOLS: YOUR WEBSITE'S DIGITAL WATCHDOG

Ever wish you had a cyber bodyguard standing at the front door of your website, scanning the crowd for troublemakers? That's basically what **EASM** tools do—**External Attack Surface Management** (a fancy term, but stick with me).

So... what *is* an EASM tool?

Think of your business like a house. You've got windows, doors, maybe even a secret tunnel (your login page, plugins, third-party services, cloud apps, and so on). EASM tools walk the perimeter of your "digital property" and let you know:

- What parts of your website and online presence are exposed to the internet
- If hackers can see vulnerable tech (like outdated software, open ports, or old login pages)
- When something new pops up that you didn't authorize (like a shadow IT tool or rogue subdomain)

In short: **EASM helps you see what the bad guys can see** —so you can fix it before they break in.

What can EASM tools protect?

- Your **website** (especially WordPress or DIY platforms)
- **Third-party tools** you connect to your site (like payment processors or CRMs)

- **Cloud-based services** or storage you forgot you signed up for (it happens to the best of us)
- **Misconfigured settings** that leave your data wide open like a screen door in a windstorm

Okay, but do I need it?

If you have a website and collect *any* kind of client data—yes. You don't need a fancy enterprise setup, either. Many EASM tools are now small business–friendly and even come baked into website security packages.

The Bottom Line

You can't fix what you don't know is broken. EASM tools like Microsoft Defender EASM and BitDefender EASM, give you that visibility—so your website isn't just online, it's protected.

If that still sounds overwhelming, don't stress. This is the stuff I help small businesses with every day. You don't have to be the tech expert—you just have to be willing to look under the hood now and then (or bring in someone who loves doing it for you).

SMART AI PRACTICES

Artificial Intelligence (AI) can be a real game-changer for small businesses, but like any powerful tool, it needs some ground rules. The first thing to remember is to be careful with what you feed into it. You wouldn't hand over your customer lists, financials, or sensitive data to a stranger, and AI tools should be treated the same way. They're great helpers, but they're not your CEO, so always keep a human in the loop to double-check the work before it goes out the door. Think of AI as your sidekick—it's there to handle the repetitive tasks like drafting, brainstorming, or sorting data so you can focus on strategy, relationships, and growth.

If you work in industries like healthcare, finance, or government contracting, you also have to pay close attention to compliance with rules like HIPAA, GLBA, or CMMC. Cutting corners with AI can create serious headaches with regulators. Even outside of compliance-heavy fields, it's smart to double-check AI's work for accuracy and bias. AI has a way of sounding confident even when it's completely wrong—kind of like that friend who swears they know the shortcut but gets you lost every time.

Security is another big factor. Since most AI platforms live in the cloud, you need to treat them like any other online account: lock them down with strong passwords, multi-factor authentication, and limit who on your team has access. When it comes to adoption, don't try to transform your entire business overnight. Start with one or two tools that solve a real problem, test them, and then scale up as you learn what works best.

Finally, be transparent with your clients. If you're using AI in your workflow, whether it's for writing, customer service, or data handling, let them know. People appreciate honesty, and it builds trust when they know there's still a human steering the ship. At the end of the day, AI is like a power tool—amazing when used correctly, but dangerous if you don't know where the "off" switch is.

FACILITY SECURITY

Physical security complements your digital efforts by protecting sensitive information stored in physical form. Even in a highly digital world, paper documents, physical drives, and office devices can become targets for theft or unauthorized access. Implementing strong facility security measures not only reduces these risks but also ensures compliance with regulatory requirements that demand the protection of sensitive physical records.

Physical security is just as important as digital safeguards. Sensitive information on printed materials and devices must be protected.

Best Practices for Facility Security

- **Control who has physical access to your devices and information:** Visitor logs, locked office doors, screen savers, etc., all help control who can see your files, even if they are electronic versions.
- **Lock Printed Materials:** Use locking file cabinets or safes for sensitive documents. Affordable options for solopreneurs working from home include small fireproof safes or space-saving locking file boxes. These solutions provide security without taking up significant space in a home office.
- **Shred Sensitive Documents:** Use cross-cut shredders or trusted shredding services for disposal.
- **Secure Electronic Disposal:** Remove hard drives before disposing of old computers, and use a professional data destruction service.

Wrapping Up

By addressing these six critical areas, you're fortifying your business against both external threats and internal errors. These protections ensure that even as the cybersecurity landscape evolves, your business remains a stronghold of safety and resilience.

Next, we'll move to the **Detect** function, where you'll learn how to identify potential threats before they escalate into serious incidents. Let's keep building your defenses!

DETECT - SPOTTING TROUBLE EARLY

Detection is not just a cybersecurity best practice; it's a legal and regulatory imperative for many industries. It helps identify threats before they escalate and ensures compliance with frameworks such as HIPAA, GLBA, PCI, CMMC, and IRS requirements. In this chapter, we'll dive deep into:

1. **Monitoring Your Systems with Affordable Tools**
2. **Recognizing Warning Signs of a Breach**
3. **Documenting Detection Efforts for Compliance**
4. **Training Employees and Yourself**

MONITORING YOUR SYSTEMS WITH AFFORDABLE TOOLS

Effective system monitoring is essential for maintaining security and meeting compliance standards. While tools like antivirus (AV), endpoint detection and response (EDR), and managed detection and response (MDR) serve distinct purposes, your choice depends on your business's size, complexity, and regulatory requirements.

Understanding AV, EDR, and MDR

- **Antivirus (AV)** software provides baseline protection by scanning for known threats like malware and spyware. It's suitable for solopreneurs or small businesses with limited resources. AV often satisfies minimum regulatory expectations, but as threats evolve, it may need to be supplemented with more advanced monitoring tools.
- **Endpoint Detection and Response (EDR)** goes deeper, constantly watching for suspicious activity across devices like unexpected file changes, unauthorized access, or zero-day exploits. This tool is essential for businesses dealing with sensitive information or operating under frameworks like HIPAA, PCI-DSS, GLBA, and CMMC.
- **Managed Detection and Response (MDR)** takes EDR a step further. With MDR, a team of cybersecurity experts monitors your systems 24/7. This is ideal for businesses that don't have in-house IT or whose regulatory obligations require constant vigilance.

If you're just getting started, begin with AV and plan to grow into EDR or MDR as your business matures or your compliance requirements become more demanding. Whichever route you take, keep logs of your monitoring efforts for at least one year—this helps satisfy audit trails required by most regulations.

Mobile Device Manager

Management should use mobile device management (MDM) software on all mobile devices to ensure the security functions listed in the section above. I highly recommend using an MDM to enforce security on mobile devices so that the user is following best practices for security and your data is protected.

Removable media (CD, DVD, flash drives, hard drives) shall be stored in a locked cabinet when not in use. The best security measures are compromised when a thumb drive with files is left on a desk for someone else to steal.

MDM or mobile device management is a software application used for managing endpoints such as laptops, smartphones, tablets etc., in a business. This software will perform many of the security functions listed in the above section. It allows the business owner to enforce security settings on devices whether owned by the business, employees, or a customers.

MDM functionality can include over-the-air distribution of applications, data, and configuration settings for all types of mobile devices, including mobile phones, smartphones, tablet computers, ruggedized mobile computers, mobile printers, mobile POS devices, etc.

Most recently, laptops and desktops have been added to the list of systems supported as mobile device management becomes more about basic device management and less about the mobile platform itself. MDM tools are leveraged for both company-owned and employee-owned (BYOD) devices across the enterprise or mobile devices owned by consumers. Consumer demand for BYOD is now requiring a greater effort for MDM and increased security for both the devices and the enterprise to which they connect, especially since employers and employees have different expectations concerning the types of restrictions that should be applied to mobile devices.

By controlling and protecting the data and configuration settings of all mobile devices in a network, MDM can reduce support costs and business risks. The intent of MDM is to optimize the functionality and security of a mobile communications network while minimizing costs and downtime.

Bring Your Own Device (BYOD)

Management should have all employees sign a BYOD Policy before connecting a personal device to the network. The fact that it is an employee-owned device makes the use of MDM even more essential. It can give the business control over data while allowing the employee the convenience of their own device for other purposes.

The policy should cover the following topics:

- Device protocols
- Restrictions on authorized use
- Privacy/company access
- Company stipend
- Safety

- Lost, stolen, hacked, or damaged equipment
- Termination of employment
- Violations of policy

RECOGNIZING WARNING SIGNS OF A BREACH

Early detection can limit the damage from a cyberattack and ensure you meet regulatory deadlines for reporting. Understanding what red flags to look for is your first line of defense.

Common indicators include unusual device behavior, like slow performance or system crashes; strange new software appearing on devices; or spikes in data usage indicating possible data exfiltration. You might also notice suspicious login activity—logins from odd times, unknown IP addresses, or multiple failed login attempts in a short period.

Understanding reporting timelines is also crucial. HIPAA requires breaches involving electronic protected health information (ePHI) to be reported within 60 days. Under GLBA, financial institutions must notify affected individuals promptly. PCI-DSS requires notifying your acquiring bank and card brands immediately, including a forensic investigation report. For CMMC, incidents involving Controlled Unclassified Information (CUI) must be reported to the Department of Defense within 72 hours. And tax professionals? The IRS mandates that you notify affected clients and the IRS as soon as possible if taxpayer data is compromised.

Compliance Requirements for Breach Reporting:

- **HIPAA:**
  - Breaches involving ePHI must be reported within 60 days.
  - Notification must go to affected individuals, the Department of Health and Human Services (HHS), and, in some cases, the media.
- **GLBA:**
  - Financial institutions must notify affected customers "as soon as possible" and report to regulatory bodies.
- **PCI-DSS:**
  - Notify your acquiring bank and relevant card brands immediately.
  - Provide a forensic investigation report detailing the breach and remediation.
- **CMMC:**
  - Incidents involving Controlled Unclassified Information (CUI) must be reported to the Department of Defense (DoD) within 72 hours.
- **IRS:**
  - Tax preparers must notify affected individuals and the IRS when taxpayer data is compromised.

Understanding these requirements ensures you stay compliant and maintain trust with stakeholders.

DOCUMENTING DETECTION EFFORTS FOR COMPLIANCE

It's not enough to detect threats; you have to prove you're doing it. Regulatory bodies want documentation to show that your detection process is active, not just theoretical.

Compliance-Required Documentation:

- **Cybersecurity Plan:** A document outlining how your organization protects and detects threats and vulnerabilities.
  - **Risk Analysis Reports:** Required to evaluate vulnerabilities in your systems.
  - **Access Logs:** Track all attempts to access systems containing cardholder data.
  - **Audit Trails:** Provide evidence of compliance with system monitoring requirements.
  - **Incident Response Plan:** A document detailing how you detect, respond to, and recover from incidents.
  - **Monitoring Logs:** Show evidence of ongoing detection efforts.
  - **Incident Reports:** Records of any security incidents detected and responses.

Best Practices for Documentation:

Make life easier by storing documentation in a centralized location using platforms like Google Workspace or Microsoft SharePoint. If you're using an EDR or MDR tool, explore its reporting capabilities—many can automate and archive these logs for you. Regular reviews of your documentation are a must. Schedule quarterly reviews and update your policies, logs, and reports to reflect on your current practices.

Training Employees and Yourself: Cybersecurity Starts with You

All the fancy tools in the world won't do much good if the people using them don't know what they're looking for—or worse, accidentally invite threats in (we're looking at you, phishing emails). Training is a cornerstone of effective detection and compliance. That means ongoing, role-based education for both employees *and* leadership. Yes, that includes you. Especially you.

Employees should be trained to recognize the signs of a cyber incident, understand what actions to take, and most importantly, know *not* to panic. Panic clicks are how ransomware parties get started. Every member of the team should know how to report suspicious activity, follow your organization's Acceptable Use Policy, and understand why it's important to update software or avoid plugging in unknown USB drives (we call those "malware on a stick").

Equally important is understanding your organization's specific cybersecurity policies. You don't need to memorize every line, but you should know where they're stored, what applies to your role, and the basic do's and don'ts. This is particularly critical for solopreneurs and micro-businesses where you wear multiple hats—especially those of the IT department.

Add cybersecurity awareness as part of onboarding and revisit it regularly with refresher training at least once a year. Need a shortcut? There are affordable platforms that offer customizable cybersecurity awareness modules—some even include short quizzes to test understanding and reinforce learning.

Bottom line: A trained team is your first line of defense. When everyone knows their role in keeping information safe, your technology tools can do what they're designed to do—*detect and protect*.

WRAPPING UP

Effective detection is more than just spotting a threat; it's about integrating monitoring tools, recognizing signs of trouble, and keeping meticulous records to satisfy compliance requirements. Whether you're using basic antivirus software or advanced MDR solutions, staying vigilant helps protect your business and its sensitive data.

Next, in **Chapter 8: Respond**, we'll explore how to take decisive action when incidents occur, ensuring minimal disruption to your operations.

RESPOND - HANDLING CYBER INCIDENTS LIKE A PRO

Even with strong cybersecurity defenses in place, no business is completely immune to a breach. That's why it's essential to prepare for the inevitable by having a structured response plan. This chapter focuses on how to handle cyber incidents like a pro—swiftly, calmly, and effectively. By understanding the different types of breaches, creating a solid Incident Response Plan (IRP), and learning how to communicate during a crisis, you'll be equipped to minimize the damage and protect your business.

TYPES OF BREACHES

Cyber incidents come in different flavors, and understanding them is key to mounting the right response. Physical breaches occur in the real world—think burglaries, stolen equipment, or someone misplacing a laptop or backup tape. Even donating or recycling old devices without properly wiping them clean can be risky. These situations can introduce unauthorized devices into your systems or lead to exposure of sensitive data.

Then there are network and system security breaches, which involve unauthorized access to your digital systems. This can include malware infections, hackers gaining access through remote connections, or even trusted employees going rogue. These breaches might compromise firewalls, routers, or other critical systems within or beyond your organizational boundaries.

Finally, data breaches involve the unauthorized exposure of sensitive information. These can result from either physical or network security incidents, or even something as simple (and dangerous) as a misconfigured file share that leaves confidential information open to the public.

PLAN FOR THEFT OR LOSS

Loss or theft of data isn't just a tech problem; it's a business problem that can damage your brand, scare away customers, and land you in hot water with regulators. Every business, regardless of size, needs to know what laws apply to them and be prepared to act fast. That's where your data breach response plan comes into play.

Your plan should include clear instructions for employees and contractors: any data loss or theft, no matter how small, must be reported immediately. Even if someone simply misplaces a backup drive, it might still be a breach. And when sensitive data is involved, hoping it turns up isn't an option—it's time to act.

Depending on the nature of the breach, you may also be required to notify local law enforcement or government agencies. If customer information is exposed, informing those affected and documenting the data lost—as well as your response measures—will be essential steps.

CREATING AN INCIDENT RESPONSE PLAN (IRP)

An Incident Response Plan (IRP) is your business's playbook for managing cybersecurity incidents. Whether or not your business is required to have one under regulation, having a documented IRP is a smart and proactive move. It saves time, money, and panic when things go sideways.

An IRP helps define who does what during an incident, what steps should be taken, and how to communicate both internally and externally. It prepares you to deal with law enforcement, regulatory bodies, and customers. It also minimizes downtime, reduces financial damage, and builds trust with customers.

Compliance standards such as HIPAA, GLBA, PCI-DSS, CMMC, and IRS Safeguard Rules all require businesses handling sensitive data to have an IRP in place. Even if you're not legally required, having an IRP puts you ahead of the game.

An effective IRP typically includes five main phases:

1. **Preparation**: Identify critical data and systems. Define roles and responsibilities—even if you're a one-person shop. Implement monitoring tools like

endpoint detection and response (EDR) and train staff to report suspicious activity.

2. **Detection and Analysis**: Establish how you'll detect threats and determine their impact. Use monitoring and alerting systems to spot anomalies and document incident details thoroughly.

3. **Containment**: Act fast to stop the spread. Short-term tactics might include disconnecting infected machines, while long-term containment could involve patching vulnerabilities or segmenting networks.

4. **Eradication and Recovery**: Remove the threat completely, identify the root cause, and restore systems using clean, verified backups. Be cautious; malware loves to hitch a ride on backups too, so scan thoroughly before restoring.

5. **Post-Incident Review**: Hold a "lessons learned" meeting to assess what went right, what went wrong, and how you can do better next time. Update your IRP based on these findings.

CONTAINING AND MITIGATING DAMAGE

When a cyber incident strikes, every second counts. The first step is to detect and isolate the threat. Use your antivirus software to sweep for known malware and rely on EDR tools for deeper insights. If you have managed detection and response (MDR) services in place, they can take the lead on monitoring and investigating threats around the clock.

Immediately disconnect affected systems from the network to prevent the threat from spreading. Then assess the scope of the breach. Figure out which data and systems have been compromised and prioritize what needs immediate attention.

Containment may involve disabling user accounts, segmenting parts of your network, or applying emergency patches. After that, neutralize the threat completely. Remove malicious code, apply security updates, and only restore systems from backups you know are clean.

Finally, communicate. Notify regulators, customers, and partners as needed. Transparency is key—not only does it fulfill your legal obligations, but it also helps maintain trust.

COMMUNICATING DURING A CRISIS

Clear communication during a crisis can make or break your response. First, identify your key stakeholders; this includes your internal team, external customers, vendors, regulators, and sometimes even the media.

Create a notification plan based on applicable regulations. For example:

- **HIPAA:** Notify affected individuals, HHS, and the media (if 500+ people are affected).
- **GLBA:** Notify customers and regulators as soon as possible.
- **PCI-DSS:** Contact your acquiring bank and payment card brands immediately.

- **CMMC:** Report incidents involving CUI to the DoD within 72 hours.
- **IRS Safeguard Rules:** Notify the IRS if taxpayer data has been compromised.

Stick to the facts in your messaging. Tell people what happened, what you're doing about it, and what they should do. Avoid speculation and keep your messages concise. Follow up regularly as you learn more, and let everyone know how you're preventing future incidents.

KEY DISASTER RECOVERY PRINCIPLES

Being prepared before disaster strikes is the best way to reduce downtime and limit damage. Identify key systems and information assets critical to your business operations and protect them using a combination of onsite and offsite backups. Natural disasters, theft, or ransomware—any of these can knock out your data, so redundancy is your friend.

Educate employees on security best practices and teach them how to retrieve data in the event of a loss. Since small businesses often operate with limited resources, every employee should understand the basics of recovery procedures.

Test your recovery plan regularly, especially after any major system changes. If you can't test frequently, at least review your disaster recovery plan quarterly to keep it up to date.

It's far more cost-effective to invest in security now than to deal with the financial and reputational fallout of a breach.

An ounce of prevention is worth a whole server room full of cure.

CYBER LIABILITY INSURANCE

To add another layer of protection, consider investing in cyber liability insurance. It can help cover costs related to identity theft, lawsuits, data recovery, and more. Data breach insurance is more focused and may be suitable for smaller operations, while full-blown cyber liability insurance offers broader protection, especially for businesses handling sensitive data or large customer bases.

Cyber liability insurance covers expenses related to data breaches and other cyberattacks on your company. These costs may include:

- Client notification
- Credit monitoring services for your business
- Forensic services to identify the source
- Public relations campaigns and goodwill marketing
- Lost income if your business has to pause operations
- Ransom in the case of cyber extortion

For expert advice, check out https://www.goetz2uinsur ance.com and speak to Anna. Mention code "CS4B"—she understands the unique needs of small business owners when it comes to cyber coverage.

NOTIFY LAW ENFORCEMENT IF NECESSARY

Depending on the type of breach and the type of business, your company may be required to notify local law enforcement or other government authorities upon discovery of a data breach. In the event of exposure of customer information, you should notify the customer(s) of the incident, record the data that was lost or exposed, and document the measures taken to ensure against future exposure.

WRAPPING UP

Cybersecurity isn't about stopping every single attack; it's about how well you respond when one gets through. With a solid IRP, quick containment, smart communication, and a strong recovery plan, your business can withstand incidents and come out stronger on the other side. Responding well can turn a potentially catastrophic event into a story of resilience and professionalism.

In the next chapter, **Recover**, we'll discuss how to rebuild more strongly after an incident, ensuring your business is back on its feet and better prepared for the future.

RECOVER – BOUNCING BACK STRONGER

The recovery phase is not just about getting back to normal; it's about coming out the other side better prepared, more resilient, and cyber-stronger. Think of it like a boxer getting knocked down in the ring—you don't just dust off and stand up; you learn how to avoid that punch next time. In this chapter, we explore the key elements of recovery after a cyber-security incident, focusing on the essentials of backup and restore, the value of conducting post-mortem reviews, and the steps required to rebuild customer trust.

BACKUP AND RESTORE ESSENTIALS

A robust backup and restore strategy is the backbone of any serious recovery plan. When disaster strikes—whether it's ransomware, hardware failure, or accidental deletion—your backups might be the only thing between your business and a data doomsday.

Backing up data is essential for three major reasons. First, it protects against data loss, especially in cyberattacks where data may be encrypted or destroyed. Second, it enables business continuity, ensuring operations can resume quickly with minimal downtime and financial disruption. And third, it's often required by law, with regulations like HIPAA, GLBA, and GDPR mandating secure backup and restore procedures.

There are several types of backups that businesses should understand. A full backup involves copying all data, which is thorough but time-consuming and requires heavy storage. Incremental backups save only the data that changed since the last backup, making them efficient but reliant on a chain of backups for full restoration. Differential backups record changes since the last full backup, striking a balance between speed and storage.

Implementing backup best practices is crucial. The 3-2-1 rule remains the gold standard: keep three copies of your data, on two different media types, with one stored offsite or in the cloud. This way, even if one copy gets corrupted or one device fails, you have a fallback. Encryption is also key; your backups should be encrypted both at rest and in transit to prevent unauthorized access. Tools like BitLocker, VeraCrypt, and encrypted cloud services are solid options.

Automating your backups removes the risk of human forgetfulness. Software like Acronis True Image, Veeam, or even built-in tools in Windows and macOS can help schedule regular backups. But don't stop there. Regularly test your restoration process. There's nothing worse than thinking you're covered, only to find out your backup is corrupted when you need it most. Simulated recovery drills can save your bacon when real incidents occur.

Cloud-based solutions offer flexible and scalable backup options. Services from AWS, Microsoft Azure, and Google Cloud offer enterprise-grade solutions with compliance features baked in. Finally, document everything. Your backup and recovery process should be clearly outlined with step-by-step instructions, login credentials, configurations, and schedules. If something happens to you or your IT person, someone else needs to be able to step in.

By treating backup and restoration as a foundational process, not an afterthought, businesses can recover swiftly and confidently from setbacks.

LEARNING FROM INCIDENTS: POST-MORTEM REVIEWS

A cybersecurity incident can feel like a gut punch, but it also offers a valuable opportunity to grow stronger. Conducting a postmortem review allows an organization to analyze what happened, pinpoint what went wrong, and figure out how to prevent it from happening again.

Postmortems serve several purposes. They help identify the root cause of an incident, reveal system and process vulnerabilities, and develop concrete steps to prevent recurrence. They also encourage accountability by clearly assigning ownership of tasks and improvements.

A thorough postmortem should start with an incident timeline. Document the sequence of events in detail, from initial detection to full recovery. Tools like Trello, Jira, or incident management platforms can help visualize these timelines.

Next is the impact assessment. You need to quantify the damage, whether it's financial loss, system downtime, or a hit to your reputation. Create structured reports that include metrics like recovery time, affected systems, and number of impacted users or clients.

Root cause analysis is the heart of the review. Use techniques like the "5 Whys" to drill down into why the incident occurred. Keep asking why until you get to the source—whether it's outdated software, poor password policies, or a phishing email that someone clicked on.

Capture the lessons learned. What worked well in your response? What didn't? Break these insights down into technical failures, procedural flaws, and human errors. Then turn those lessons into actionable recommendations. Assign each one to a responsible team member and set deadlines to ensure follow-through.

Disseminate your findings across the organization. Share insights with stakeholders and integrate them into employee training programs. Workshops and team briefings can reinforce key takeaways.

For a postmortem to be effective, build a cross-functional team that includes IT, legal, public relations, and leadership. You want a 360-degree view of what went down. Create a safe, blame-free environment where people can speak openly. Anonymous surveys can help if folks are hesitant to share mistakes.

Finally, document everything. From the minute the incident starts to the final wrap-up meeting, keep detailed records. Store them securely and make sure they're accessible for future reference. Use project management tools to track the implementation of your recommendations.

When done right, postmortem reviews are not just a recovery step; they're a launchpad for strengthening your entire cybersecurity posture.

REBUILDING CUSTOMER TRUST AFTER AN INCIDENT

Trust is like a mirror—once cracked, it's hard to fix. After a cybersecurity incident, businesses must work overtime to restore customer confidence. It's not just about fixing the tech. It's about managing emotions, reputations, and relationships.

Trust matters because it directly impacts customer retention, brand reputation, and compliance obligations. Mishandling your response can drive customers away and attract regulatory scrutiny.

Rebuilding starts with communication. Notify customers promptly with clear, honest information about the incident. Don't sugarcoat or delay; transparency earns respect. Having pre-written notification templates can help you respond quickly and consistently.

Next, own it. Publicly acknowledge what happened and what you're doing to make things right. Whether through a CEO statement, a press release, or a social media update, showing accountability builds credibility.

Offer resources to affected individuals. Credit monitoring, identity theft protection, and dedicated hotlines provide practical help and show you care. Partner with services like Experian or LifeLock to deliver professional support.

Detail the steps you're taking to prevent a repeat incident. Are you rolling out new technologies? Updating policies? Providing staff training? Say so. Publishing an updated security policy or a post-incident report shows your commitment to improvement.

Keep the lines of communication open. Don't go dark after the initial announcement. Provide regular updates, FAQs, and access to support staff. Hosting webinars or Q&A sessions can help answer lingering concerns.

Invite feedback. Ask customers how you're doing. Use surveys to gauge satisfaction with your response and recovery. It may sting, but the insights are invaluable for improvement.

Take the infamous 2017 Equifax breach as a cautionary tale. Their delayed notification and vague responses eroded public trust for years. On the flip side, companies that communicate swiftly, transparently, and empathetically often find their customer base more loyal after recovery than before.

Long-term, focus on building a customer-centric culture that emphasizes data security. Launch marketing campaigns that reinforce your commitment to protecting information. Work with third-party organizations that can certify your security practices and help rebuild credibility.

Recovering from a breach is not just about damage control. It's about relationship repair and trust reconstruction. Done well, it can even become a differentiator in your brand story.

WRAPPING UP

Recovering from a cybersecurity incident is never easy, but it's a golden opportunity to strengthen your systems, educate your team, and reinforce customer relationships. With solid backup strategies, a commitment to learning through post-mortem reviews, and a transparent approach to customer communication, businesses can not only bounce back—they can bounce back stronger.

TOOLS AND RESOURCES

In today's cybersecurity landscape, solopreneurs and small businesses face the daunting challenge of protecting sensitive information without the benefit of large IT teams or deep-pocket budgets. The good news? You don't need a million-dollar setup to stay cyber safe. With the right tools, simple checklists, and a few rock-solid policies, you can guard your data like a pro. This chapter introduces affordable and user-friendly cybersecurity tools, actionable cybersecurity checklists, and downloadable policy templates to simplify compliance and enhance your security posture. Whether you're navigating the requirements of GLBA, HIPAA, or just trying to sleep better at night knowing your data is locked down, you're in the right place.

AFFORDABLE AND EFFECTIVE CYBERSECURITY TOOLS

Why Tools Matter: Let's be real: doing everything manually is like trying to bail water out of a sinking boat with a thimble. Cybersecurity tools automate the grunt work, help you stay consistent, and—best of all—save time and money. With the rise of free and open-source solutions, even the smallest business can lock things down like Fort Knox. Plus, many of these tools are now designed with compliance in mind, helping you meet requirements from regulations like HIPAA and GLBA without needing to decipher a government manual in your spare time.

Essential Cybersecurity Tools:

• **Password Managers:** Simplify password management by generating and securely storing strong passwords. Enable MFA (multi-factor authentication) for an added layer of security and assign admin controls to ensure only approved users access certain vaults.

• **Virtual Private Networks (VPNs):** Encrypts internet connections, protecting data from interception on public Wi-Fi. Always activate the VPN before accessing sensitive information remotely and configure auto-connect settings to minimize human error.

• **Backup Solutions:** Protects against data loss from ransomware, hardware failures, or human errors. Evaluate cloud-based solutions; these services support HIPAA and GLBA compliance when configured properly. Or go old school and buy an encrypted external hard drive for local backups. Best practice? Do both. Follow the 3-2-1 backup rule for maximum data protection—3 copies of your data, 2 different media types, 1 stored offsite.

• **Endpoint Protection:** Guards devices against malware, phishing, and other cyber threats. Use a Managed Detection and Response (MDR) solution; these offer HIPAA and GLBA compliance support. Schedule regular scans, enable real-time protection, and monitor dashboards for anomalies. Keep all definitions and software updated automatically.

• **Email Security Solutions:** Prevents phishing, spam, and malicious email links. Consider tools that offer HIPAA-compliant email encryption and phishing detection. Train employees and contractors to identify suspicious emails and configure alerts for attempted impersonations.

• **Monitoring and Incident Response Tools:** Provides real-time alerts and tracks security events. Tools that offer logging, monitoring, and incident reporting are aligned with HIPAA and GLBA. Customize alerts to focus on high-risk incidents and schedule regular log reviews.

CYBERSECURITY CHECKLISTS FOR SOLOPRENEURS

Why Checklists Work: In a world full of distractions, cyber-security checklists bring order to chaos. They break down complex tasks into bite-sized, actionable steps. That's not just convenient; it's critical when compliance is on the line. Checklists also help you maintain consistency across daily, weekly, and monthly security practices. Best of all, they're scalable, meaning you can build a security program that grows right alongside your business.

Actionable Steps for Each NIST CSF Function:

• **Identify:** Conduct a full risk assessment. Inventory all hardware and software assets using spreadsheet templates or asset-tracking software. Document data flows and storage locations —know where your sensitive data lives and where it travels.

• **Protect:** Implement multi-factor authentication across all user accounts. Enforce strong password policies through a password manager. Secure physical workspaces with lockable storage and access controls. Apply software and firmware updates regularly and enable auto-patching where available.

• **Detect:** Set up alerts for unusual login attempts, unrecognized devices, or large data transfers. Enable logging on critical systems, especially those storing or processing client or financial data. Review logs weekly or use automated tools that summarize trends and flag anomalies.

• **Respond:** Create a written response plan using templates aligned with HIPAA and GLBA requirements. Assign roles and responsibilities so everyone knows who does what during an incident. Conduct quarterly incident simulations to make sure your team is ready to act.

• **Recover:** Test your backup monthly and perform full restore tests at least quarterly. Review and revise your recovery plan based on lessons learned from real incidents or simulations. Maintain documentation for regulators, including proof of regular testing and results.

Daily, Weekly, and Monthly Tasks:

Daily: Monitor dashboards for system alerts or unusual activity. Review spam or quarantine folders to catch any legitimate messages.

Weekly: Review user access logs and revoke access no longer needed. Check for updates on all software, browsers, and operating systems.

Monthly: Run a simulated phishing campaign. Verify backups are intact and stored offsite or in the cloud. Review and update your policies and incident response documentation.

RECOMMENDED POLICIES

Why Policies Are Crucial: Policies provide a structured game plan for your cybersecurity approach. They don't just tell your team what to do; they prove to regulators, clients, and vendors that you take security seriously. A solid policy framework will help you pass audits, respond to breaches, and avoid compliance fines. Whether you're protecting medical records under HIPAA or financial info under GLBA, policies keep you proactive, not reactive.

RECOMMENDED CYBERSECURITY POLICIES & WHO NEEDS THEM

- **Cybersecurity Policy**

A high-level document that defines your company's overall security objectives, responsibilities, and approach to protecting data and systems. It often references the other policies listed here.

Who Needs It: Every organization—no matter the size. This is your "mission statement" for cybersecurity and is often requested by regulators, partners, and cyber insurance providers.

Learn More: https://www.fcc.gov/cyberplanner

- **Written Information Security Program (WISP)**

A formal document that outlines your organization's cybersecurity strategy, risk management process, and protection of sensitive data.

Who Needs It: Businesses that handle nonpublic personal information (NPI)—especially financial institutions under the **GLBA Safeguards Rule,** such as accountants, tax professionals, mortgage lenders, and credit repair firms.

Learn More: https://www.irs.gov/pub/irs-pdf/p5708.pdf

- **System Security Plan (SSP)**

Describes the current security environment, including systems, controls, and responsibilities.

Who Needs It: Organizations handling **Controlled Unclassified Information (CUI)** for federal contracts under **NIST 800-171**, or those needing **CMMC** certification.

Learn More: https://csrc.nist.gov/files/pubs/sp/800/171/r2/upd1/final/docs/cui-ssp-template-final.docx

- **Plan of Action and Milestones (POA&M)**

Outlines what needs fixing, how you plan to fix it, and when it will be done. Think of it as a cybersecurity to-do list with deadlines.

Who Needs It: Federal contractors under **NIST or CMMC**, and any business trying to actively improve and track cybersecurity.

Learn More: https://csrc.nist.gov/files/pubs/sp/800/171/r2/upd1/final/docs/cui-plan-of-action-template-final.docx

- **HIPAA Privacy and Security Policies**

Covers how you access, use, store, and transmit Protected Health Information (PHI).

Who Needs It: Covered entities (like doctors and clinics) and business associates (such as billing companies, IT providers, and consultants).

Learn More: https://www.healthit.gov/sites/
default/files/resources/info_security_policy_tem
plate_v1_0.docx

- **Website Privacy Policy**

Explains how you collect, use, and store visitor data
on your website to stay on the right side of consumer
protection laws.

Who Needs It: Any business with a website
collecting personal data—especially in California
(CCPA), Virginia (VCDPA), or any of the other 20+
states enacting consumer privacy laws.

Learn More: https://docs.google.com/document/d/
1W3INZmdL8T72_HTKPXdC8L1wqXVkkwTd
Jwfyl0WppaQ/edit?tab=t.0

- **Acceptable Use Policy (AUP)**

Lays out the do's and don'ts for anyone using your
systems, devices, or internet connections.

Who Needs It: Every business with employees,
contractors, or vendors who touch your data or assets.

- **Bring Your Own Device (BYOD) Policy**

Defines the rules for using personal devices like smartphones or laptops for work tasks.

Who Needs It: Any business allowing team members to check work email or access company files on personal devices.

- **Incident Response Plan**

A playbook for what to do when things go sideways —like malware, data breaches, or system outages. It outlines roles, responsibilities, and recovery steps.

Who Needs It: Any business that stores sensitive data or relies on tech (which is pretty much all of us). Required under frameworks like **NIST**, **HIPAA**, and **PCI-DSS**.

Learn More: https://csrc.nist.gov/publications/detail/sp/800-61/rev-2/final

- **Data Breach Notification Plan**

Details how and when you must notify customers, regulators, and others if sensitive data is compromised.
Who Needs It: Every business. All 50 states, plus D.C., Puerto Rico, and other territories have their own breach notification laws.
Learn More: https://csrc.nist.gov/publications/detail/sp/800-61/rev-2/final

By implementing these tools, checklists, and policies, solopreneurs can create a robust cybersecurity framework that protects their business, builds customer trust, and ensures regulatory compliance. You don't need to be a tech wizard— just a smart operator who's ready to roll up your sleeves and build a cyber-safe culture.

MEASURING ROI AND STAYING COMPLIANT

In today's digital economy, cybersecurity is more than just an operational necessity—it's a strategic investment that protects your business, strengthens customer relationships, and ensures compliance with industry standards. Measuring the return on investment (ROI) in cybersecurity and maintaining regulatory compliance can seem daunting, but this chapter will guide you through understanding the benefits, tracking progress, and staying ahead of evolving threats and requirements.

THE ROI OF CYBERSECURITY

Why Cybersecurity Pays Off

Avoiding financial disasters is one of the most compelling reasons to invest in cybersecurity. The cost of a breach, including legal penalties, lost business, and remediation, can far exceed the cost of preventive measures. Tools like firewalls, antivirus software, and employee training are relatively affordable and can prevent catastrophic losses. For example, a data breach that could cost millions might be prevented with a modest investment in endpoint protection and regular risk assessments.

Another key benefit is protecting your business's reputation. A well-protected company fosters trust, which not only encourages customer loyalty but also attracts new clients. Customers are more likely to do business with companies they perceive as secure. Demonstrating a proactive approach to cybersecurity, such as showcasing certifications and maintaining strong policies, builds confidence and sets you apart from competitors.

Cybersecurity also enhances efficiency. Secure systems reduce downtime, which boosts productivity. Frequent cyber incidents can disrupt or even halt operations, leading to revenue loss and frustration. Automating threat detection and response processes can streamline operations and allow your team to focus on growing the business.

How Cybersecurity Builds Trust

Transparency is crucial. Sharing your cybersecurity practices with customers reinforces their confidence in your commitment to protecting their data. Regular updates on your security efforts, such as adopting new tools or completing audits, demonstrate accountability and care.

Certifications and compliance achievements, such as HIPAA compliance or PCI-DSS certification, serve as third-party validations of your dedication to security. These credentials show that your business adheres to recognized standards and is serious about safeguarding information.

Examples of ROI Metrics

Incident cost reduction is a powerful way to demonstrate ROI. Compare the costs of your cybersecurity tools against the financial impact of potential breaches. This includes calculating the average cost per incident before and after implementing new security measures.

Customer retention rates can also reflect the effectiveness of your cybersecurity efforts. Measuring how trust in your security practices influences customer loyalty—using surveys and feedback—can help you quantify the value of your investments.

Operational savings are another strong metric. Evaluate the time and resources saved through automation. For example, automated backups reduce the need for manual intervention and help prevent losses caused by human error.

TRACKING YOUR PROGRESS

Why Metrics Matter

Tracking metrics allows you to assess your current cybersecurity maturity and identify areas for improvement. Without clear benchmarks, it's hard to know whether your initiatives are working or if vulnerabilities persist. Metrics also help you demonstrate the value of your security investments to stakeholders, making it easier to gain buy-in from partners or investors by illustrating tangible results.

How to Measure Cybersecurity Maturity

Key metrics to track include the number of detected threats, which indicates the effectiveness of your monitoring tools. A consistent or decreasing number of detected threats can suggest robust defenses, while sudden spikes may point to areas needing additional attention.

Time to respond (TTR) is another important metric, measuring how quickly your team can mitigate threats. Faster response times correlate with reduced damage and lower recovery costs.

The frequency of security audits also reflects your organization's diligence. Conducting regular audits shows a commitment to continuous improvement and helps identify hidden weaknesses before they become serious issues.

Moving Up the NIST CSF Tiers

Progressing through the NIST Cybersecurity Framework (CSF) tiers can help you mature your cybersecurity program.

- In Tier 1, Partial, businesses begin by identifying assets and risks. Using tools like simple risk assessment templates helps establish a foundational understanding of your environment.
- In Tier 2, Risk-Informed, the organization develops basic policies and incorporates cybersecurity training. This stage ensures that staff understand their roles in safeguarding the business.
- Tier 3, Repeatable, focuses on automating security processes and establishing metrics for ongoing

improvement. Regularly reviewing logs and incident reports is key to refining your security approach.

- Tier 4, Adaptive, involves proactively monitoring for emerging threats and adjusting strategies dynamically. Leveraging advanced threat intelligence and participating in industry forums can help you stay ahead of cybercriminals.

Free Tools for NIST CSF Self-Assessment

1. **NIST Cybersecurity Framework Starter Kit**
   - **What it is:** An introductory resource provided by NIST to help organizations understand and begin implementing the CSF.
   - **Why it's helpful:** Offers a simplified approach to identifying and prioritizing cybersecurity activities.
   - **Where to find it:** Visit NIST's official website and look for the Starter Kit under the "Resources" section.
2. **CISA Cyber Essentials Toolkits**
   - **What it is:** A set of modules developed by the Cybersecurity and Infrastructure Security Agency (CISA) focusing on fundamental cybersecurity practices.
   - **Why it's helpful:** Provides actionable guidance tailored for small businesses and solopreneurs to enhance their cybersecurity posture.
   - **Where to find it:** Access the toolkits at CISA's Cyber Essentials.
3. **NIST Small Business Cybersecurity Corner**

- ○ **What it is:** A dedicated portal by NIST offering resources specifically for small businesses.
- ○ **Why it's helpful:** Includes guides, fact sheets, and tools that align with the NIST CSF, all tailored for small business needs.
- ○ **Where to find it:** Explore the resources at NIST Small Business Cybersecurity Corner.

4. **FTC Cybersecurity for Small Business**
   - ○ **What it is:** A resource hub by the Federal Trade Commission providing information on cybersecurity basics.
   - ○ **Why it's helpful:** Offers quizzes, videos, and guides to help small businesses understand and implement cybersecurity best practices.
   - ○ **Where to find it:** Visit FTC's Cybersecurity for Small Business.

STAYING COMPLIANT AND ADAPTING TO CHANGE

Why Compliance Is Critical:

Let's delve into the potential fines associated with non-compliance in key cybersecurity regulations, focusing on HIPAA, FTC regulations, and PCI DSS. Understanding these penalties is crucial for solopreneurs and small business owners to appreciate the importance of maintaining compliance.

HIPAA (Health Insurance Portability and Accountability Act)

The U.S. Department of Health and Human Services (HHS) enforces HIPAA regulations, which protect sensitive patient health information. Penalties for non-compliance are tiered based on the level of negligence:

- **Tier 1:** Unknowing violations can result in fines ranging from $141 to $35,581 per violation, with an annual maximum of $35,581.
- **Tier 2:** Violations due to reasonable cause, not willful neglect, can incur fines from $1,424 to $71,162 per violation, with an annual maximum of $142,355.
- **Tier 3:** Violations due to willful neglect that are corrected within a specified time frame can lead to fines from $14,232 to $71,162 per violation, with an annual maximum of $355,808.
- **Tier 4:** Violations due to willful neglect that are not corrected can result in fines of $71,162 per violation, with an annual maximum of $2,134,831.

The tiers of criminal penalties for HIPAA violations are:

- **Tier 1**: Reasonable cause or no knowledge of violation – Up to 1 year in jail
- **Tier 2**: Obtaining PHI under false pretenses – Up to 5 years in jail
- **Tier 3**: Obtaining PHI for personal gain or with malicious intent – Up to 10 years in jail

These penalties underscore the importance of proactive compliance measures.

FTC Regulations

The Federal Trade Commission (FTC) enforces regulations to protect consumers' personal information. Violations can lead to significant penalties.

- **Health Breach Notification Rule:** Failure to notify affected individuals and the FTC of a data breach involving personal health records can result in fines of up to $53,088 per violation.
- **General Data Protection Violations:** Engaging in unfair or deceptive practices related to consumer data can also attract fines up to $53,088 per violation.

These penalties highlight the necessity of transparent and secure data handling practices.

PCI DSS (Payment Card Industry Data Security Standard)

While PCI DSS compliance is enforced by payment card brands rather than a federal agency, non-compliance can still result in substantial consequences.

- **Fines:** Payment processors may impose fines ranging from $5,000 to $100,000 per month for non-compliance.
- **Increased Transaction Fees:** Non-compliant businesses may face higher transaction fees.

- **Termination of Merchant Account:** Continued non-compliance can lead to the termination of the ability to process credit card payments.

These repercussions emphasize the importance of adhering to PCI DSS standards to maintain the ability to process payment cards securely.

In Summary:

Non-compliance with cybersecurity regulations can lead to severe financial penalties and operational disruptions. For solopreneurs and small business owners, investing in compliance is not just a legal obligation but a critical component of business sustainability and customer trust.

Compliance also signals to customers and partners that your business is professional and trustworthy. It demonstrates that you take the security of sensitive information seriously and follow industry best practices.

How to Stay Compliant:

Staying up to date with regulatory changes is key. Subscribe to newsletters from governing bodies like the FTC, HHS, or NIST to receive timely updates and guidance. Joining professional associations focused on cybersecurity and compliance can also provide access to valuable resources and peer support.

Developing an audit schedule is another crucial step. Regular audits help ensure ongoing compliance and prepare you for any external inspections. Governance, Risk, and Compliance (GRC) platforms can simplify the audit process by centralizing your compliance documentation and tracking requirements.

To adapt to emerging threats, stay informed through alerts from sources like the Cybersecurity and Infrastructure Security Agency (CISA), which offers actionable advice tailored to current threat trends. Annual reviews of your cybersecurity policies and practices help ensure they stay relevant and effective as your business evolves.

Free Cybersecurity Training & Resources from the National Cybersecurity Alliance

1. **Cybersecurity for Business Hub**
   - This section offers practical guides, toolkits, and articles designed specifically for small businesses. Topics include managing cyber risks, improving cyber resilience, and protecting business social media accounts. These resources are crafted to be actionable and easy to implement. https://www.staysafeonline.org/resources/cybersecurity-for-business?

2. **Security Awareness Episodes**
   - A series of eight short, engaging videos that cover essential cybersecurity topics such as password management and phishing awareness. These videos are ideal for self-paced learning and can also be shared with employees or clients. https://www.staysafeonline.org/articles/security-awareness-episodes?

3. **Career and Education Resources**

- The NCA provides links to various educational tools, including the Cyber Career Pathways Tool from NICCS. This tool helps individuals explore different roles within the cybersecurity field and identify the skills needed for each. https://www.staysafeonline.org/resources/career-and-education?

4. **Interactive Cybersecurity Training Modules**
   - Through partnerships, the NCA offers access to hands-on cybersecurity training modules. These modules are designed to enhance practical skills and are available for free. https://www.staysafeonline.org/articles/sans-institute-free-cyber-security-training?

5. **Volunteer Toolkit**
   - For those interested in promoting cybersecurity awareness, the NCA provides a toolkit with downloadable resources such as tip sheets, social media graphics, and sample communications. This is particularly useful for solopreneurs looking to educate their networks. https://www.staysafeonline.org/articles/teach-others-how-to-stay-safe-online-volunteer-toolkit?

These resources are designed to be user-friendly and require no prior technical expertise, making them ideal for solopreneurs and small business owners seeking to enhance their cybersecurity knowledge and practices.

WRAPPING IT UP

Cybersecurity and compliance are not static goals but ongoing processes that evolve with technology and emerging threats. By understanding the ROI of cybersecurity, tracking progress, and staying compliant, you can protect your business, strengthen customer trust, and set yourself up for long-term success. With the tools, metrics, and resources outlined in this chapter, you will be prepared to adapt to the ever-changing cybersecurity landscape and continue thriving on your entrepreneurial journey.

CONCLUSION

CYBERSECURITY DOESN'T HAVE TO BE COMPLICATED—IT JUST HAS TO BE INTENTIONAL

If you're reading this conclusion, I want to pause and give you some major credit: most folks never finish what they start. But you? You stuck with it, chapter after chapter, proving that you're serious about protecting your business, your clients, and your livelihood. That alone puts you ahead of the game.

Let's take a moment to look back at what you've just accomplished. You've gone from "I don't even know where to start" to "Hey, I've got a handle on this cybersecurity thing!" And if you still don't feel one hundred percent confident—good. That means you care enough to keep learning and growing.

Cybersecurity isn't a destination. It's a journey. (Yeah, I know —it sounds like a bumper sticker, but it's true.) There will always be new threats, evolving tech, and cybercriminals trying to outsmart you. But thanks to the **NIST Cybersecu-**

rity Framework 2.0, you now have a flexible, scalable system that grows with your business. Whether you're a solopreneur running your empire from the kitchen table or a growing micro-business juggling staff and clients, the tools are in your hands.

YOU'VE BUILT A CYBER MINDSET

Throughout this book, we didn't just throw tech terms at you. We focused on building **a cyber-safe mindset**—because that's what truly protects you. Fancy software is nice. Firewalls and encryption help. But if you and your team don't understand the *why* behind your security habits, it's like locking the front door and leaving the windows wide open.

You learned to identify your data, lock it down, detect when something's wrong, and respond like a pro. You now understand governance isn't just corporate-speak—it's setting the rules and culture that guide your security efforts. And you've seen how protecting your business is just as much about behavior as it is about tech.

Culture beats technology every time. ✺

SOLOPRENEURS AND SMALL BUSINESSES: YOU ARE THE TARGET

Let's keep it real: you're a target. I know that sounds dramatic, but hackers love going after the little guys. Why? Because they assume you won't have strong defenses. They think you're too busy, too under-resourced, or too "non-techy" to notice something fishy until it's too late.

But you're not just a target—you're now a **harder** target.

You've got a better understanding of what hackers are after, how they'll try to get in, and what you can do to stop them. You've even started thinking like a Chief Information Security Officer (CISO)—just one who wears a lot of hats and probably drinks more coffee than is healthy ☕.

WHAT SUCCESS LOOKS LIKE FROM HERE

Success doesn't mean never getting attacked. Success means being prepared. It means catching the phishing email before clicking. It means having a backup ready when ransomware shows up. It means knowing what data you hold, who has access, and how you'll respond if things go sideways.

Let me give you a quick checklist of what cyber success might look like:

- You've documented your policies—even if they're short and simple.
- Your passwords don't all include your dog's name and birth year.
- Your software is updated, your data is backed up, and your Wi-Fi has a decent password (not "password123" 😶).
- You've trained your team—even if it's just you and your teenager helping with email.
- You know the steps to take if a breach happens—and you won't panic.

If any of that still feels overwhelming, remember: **progress, not perfection.** Every little improvement matters.

DON'T FORGET THE HUMAN SIDE

Technology gets the spotlight, but humans are the real MVPs —or the weakest link, depending on the day. That's why this book focused so much on behavior, culture, and awareness. Cybersecurity is something you *do*, not just something you *buy*.

Train yourself. Train your team. Talk about security. Make it normal, not scary. It's like washing your hands—you don't need to be a doctor to do it right, but if you skip it, things get messy fast.

CYBERSECURITY IS A BUSINESS ADVANTAGE

Here's the good news most small business owners don't realize: getting cyber-safe gives you a *competitive edge*.

Your customers, clients, and partners want to trust you. They want to know their info is safe in your hands. By following the NIST CSF and building that culture of security, you're telling them, "I take your trust seriously."

And if you ever want to scale, apply for contracts, work with the government, or even partner with larger businesses—your cybersecurity practices could be the difference between "Let's go with them" and "Thanks, but no thanks."

KEEP THE MOMENTUM GOING

Now what?

- **Revisit this book regularly.** Don't let it collect digital dust on your desktop.
- **Update your policies and tools annually.** Make cybersecurity part of your business calendar.
- **Stay curious.** Subscribe to cybersecurity newsletters, follow updates from NIST, or check in with folks like me who stay in the trenches so you don't have to.
- **Ask for help when you need it.** You're not alone, and there are people (like me 🌸) who specialize in helping solopreneurs and small businesses do this without going broke or bonkers.

MY MISSION IS YOUR SUCCESS

I wrote this book because I've seen firsthand what happens when small businesses get hit and don't have a plan. It's frustrating. It's avoidable. And worst of all—it's preventable with the *right guidance.*

I created Cybersecurity4biz for people like you—hard-working, passionate solopreneurs and micro business owners who don't want to get bogged down in tech jargon but do want to protect what they've built.

So whether you're a bookkeeper, a healthcare provider, a coach, a content creator, or anything in between: your data matters. Your clients' trust matters. Your peace of mind matters.

FINAL WORDS (BEFORE THE CYBER ALARM CLOCK RINGS)

Let's be honest—this stuff isn't always fun. You'd probably rather be working with clients, building your brand, or sipping coffee on the porch. But cybersecurity doesn't have to be a burden. When done right, it becomes part of how you do business. Quiet. Consistent. Smart.

You're the boss. Now you're also the CISO. And the good news is—you're doing just fine.

So take a breath. Give yourself a high five. And remember:

Cybersecurity isn't about fear—it's about **freedom**.

Freedom to run your business with confidence.

Freedom to grow without chaos.

Freedom to sleep at night knowing your data is protected.

You've now got the tools, tips, and mindset to start building a stronger, cyber-safe business—but reading is only the first step. The next one is *action*.

If you're unsure where to begin or want to see how your current setup measures up, don't go it alone. I'm offering a **free cybersecurity assessment** for readers of this book.

No strings, no pressure—just practical insight from someone who's been in the trenches.

Visit
https://www.cybersecurity4biz.com/free-assessments
and take that first step toward securing your data, your
business, and your peace of mind.

**Want help getting started or need a second set of eyes
on your cyber safety plan?**

Visit **www.Cybersecurity4biz.com** or
email **Todd directly at
consultant@cybersecurity4biz.com**

Now go secure the heck out of your business.

You've got this. 💪

A PERSONAL REQUEST

Thank you so much for reading *The Small Business Owner's Cybersecurity Guide*. I wrote this book to help solopreneurs, entrepreneurs, and small business owners like you feel confident about protecting your business and clients online.

If you find this guide helpful, the best way you can support me is by leaving an **honest review on Amazon**. Your feedback not only helps me improve, but it also helps other small business owners discover the tools they need to stay cyber safe.

It only takes a minute, and it makes a huge difference. 🙏

Leave Your Review Here:
https://www.amazon.com/review/create-review/?asin=
B0FRYLKTXV

📱 Or simply scan the QR code on the next page

Why Your Review Matters

✅ Helps other small business owners find the book

✅ Gives real-world feedback that helps me improve

✅ Spreads the mission of building a **cyber-safe culture**

Thank you for your support—and for being part of the movement to make small businesses stronger, safer, and more resilient online.

— Todd Mitchell

GLOSSARY OF ACRONYMS

- **AI** - Artificial Intelligence
- **CISA** – Cybersecurity and Infrastructure Security Agency
- **CISO** – Chief Information Security Officer
- **CMMC** – Cybersecurity Maturity Model Certification
- **CRM** – Customer Relationship Management
- **CSF** – Cybersecurity Framework (NIST CSF)
- **CVV** – Card Verification Value (credit/debit card security code)
- **EASM** – External Attack Surface Management
- **EDR** – Endpoint Detection and Response
- **EMR** – Electronic Medical Record
- **FCRA** – Fair Credit Reporting Act
- **FTC** – Federal Trade Commission
- **GDPR** – General Data Protection Regulation
- **GLBA** – Gramm-Leach-Bliley Act
- **HHS** – U.S. Department of Health and Human Services

- **HIPAA** – Health Insurance Portability and Accountability Act
- **HITECH** – Health Information Technology for Economic and Clinical Health Act
- **IRP** – Incident Response Plan
- **IRS** – Internal Revenue Service
- **IT** – Information Technology
- **MDM** – Mobile Device Management
- **MDR** – Managed Detection and Response
- **MFA** – Multi-Factor Authentication
- **NAS** – Network Attached Storage
- **NIST** – National Institute of Standards and Technology
- **NPI** – Non-Public Personal Information
- **PCI DSS** – Payment Card Industry Data Security Standard
- **PHI** – Protected Health Information
- **PII** – Personally Identifiable Information
- **PIN** – Personal Identification Number
- **RBAC** – Role-Based Access Control
- **ROI** – Return on Investment
- **SIM** – Subscriber Identity Module
- **SMS** – Short Message Service
- **SP** – Special Publication (usually NIST SP)
- **SSN** – Social Security Number
- **SSP** – System Security Plan
- **VPN** – Virtual Private Network
- **WISP** – Written Information Security Program

ACKNOWLEDGMENTS

My publishing coach, Melanie Sterling, whose wisdom, patience, and guidance helped transform scattered thoughts into a structured vision. Your steady hand steered this project toward completion.

My editor, Lesa Boutin, whose skill and keen eye brought clarity and life to these pages. Your dedication ensured that every word carried weight and purpose.

ABOUT THE AUTHOR

Todd Mitchell, owner of **Cybersecurity4biz LLC** (a Disabled Veteran-Owned Small Business), is a retired U.S. Navy veteran and cybersecurity expert with over 30 years of experience protecting sensitive information. With degrees in IT, ethical hacking, an MBA, and a Master's in Cybersecurity Policy, Todd is dedicated to helping small businesses and families stay cyber safe.

He has contributed to the NIST SP 800 series and helped shape cybersecurity controls for the Department of Defense, government agencies, and industries like healthcare and finance. As part of the NIST Small Business Cybersecurity Community of Interest, Todd shares insights to support the unique cybersecurity needs of small businesses.

The inspiration for Cybersecurity4biz came when Todd was leading software design for the U.S. Marine Corps Command and Control systems and implementing cybersecurity for the Department of Defense. Around that time, a friend—a DJ— was hacked and lost his entire music library. When Todd was asked to help, he searched everywhere for a cybersecurity provider for small businesses, only to find that no one would work with companies with fewer than 250 computers.

Realizing there was a massive gap in support, Todd knew most solopreneurs and micro-businesses couldn't afford (and didn't need) enterprise-level solutions. With a nudge from his friend, he left the corporate world to launch Cybersecurity4biz, offering practical, affordable cybersecurity solutions tailored for the little guy. His mission? *The little guy helping the little guy.*

Todd runs his business from home and practices what he preaches—securing his own network while safeguarding client data, even amidst the chaos of family IoT devices like smart TVs, cat feeders, and that one "helpful" doorbell.

Outside of cybersecurity, Todd is married to his beautiful wife, Tammy, and is a proud father to an amazing daughter and two awesome grandchildren. He's a self-proclaimed old-school nerd who enjoys rolling real dice in classic Dungeons & Dragons sessions, and when not working, he loves hitting the open road in his RV and exploring national parks across the country.